Exchange Rate Politics
in Latin America

Carol Wise
Riordan Roett
EDITORS

Exchange Rate Politics
in Latin America

BROOKINGS INSTITUTION PRESS
Washington, D.C.

332.456
E962
c. 2

ABOUT BROOKINGS

The Brookings Institution is a private nonprofit organization devoted to research, education, and publication on important issues of domestic and foreign policy. Its principal purpose is to bring knowledge to bear on current and emerging policy problems. The Institution maintains a position of neutrality on issues of public policy. Interpretations or conclusions in Brookings publications should be understood to be solely those of the authors.

Copyright © 2000
THE BROOKINGS INSTITUTION
1775 Massachusetts Avenue, N.W., Washington, D.C. 20036
www.brookings.edu

All rights reserved

Library of Congress Cataloging-in-Publication data

Exchange rate politics in Latin America / Carol Wise and Riordan Roett, editors.
    p.   cm.
Includes bibliographical references and index.
   ISBN 0-8157-9487-8 (pbk.: alk. paper)
   1. Foreign exchange rates—Government policy—Latin America—Case studies.   2. Foreign exchange rates—Political aspects—Latin America—Case studies.   I. Wise, Carol.   II. Roett, Riordan.
   HG3915.5 .E83 2000   00-010111
   352.4'56'098—dc21   CIP

9 8 7 6 5 4 3 2 1

The paper used in this publication meets minimum requirements of the American National Standard for Information Sciences—Permanence of Paper for Printed Library Materials: ANSI Z39.48-1984.

Typeset in Adobe Garamond

Composition by R. Lynn Rivenbark
Macon, Georgia

Printed by R. R. Donnelley and Sons
Harrisonburg, Virginia

Contents

University Libraries
Carnegie Mellon University
Pittsburgh, PA 15213-3890

v

Acknowledgments

W E OWE WARM THANKS to our fellow authors and to the other colleagues who participated in the study group meetings organized to discuss the themes of this volume, particularly those who traveled from Canada, Mexico, and other parts of the United States and the hemisphere. We would also like to acknowledge Guadalupe Paz, the assistant director for projects in the SAIS Western Hemisphere Program, for her superb effort in coordinating this project from beginning to end and for preparing the final manuscript. Donna Verdier was instrumental in the editing process, and we would like to express our gratitude for her patience and skillful work.

At Brookings Institution Press, we extend thanks to Robin DuBlanc for editing the final manuscript, Carlotta Ribar for proofreading the pages, and Shirley Kessel for providing the index.

Finally, we owe our deepest gratitude to the Tinker Foundation for its generous support and for making this project possible.

CAROL WISE
RIORDAN ROETT

*Exchange Rate Politics
in Latin America*

1

CAROL WISE

Introduction: Debates, Performance, and the Politics of Policy Choice

JUST AS THE Great Depression of the 1930s triggered dramatic economic and political changes in Latin America, so too did the next major regionwide downturn—the 1982 debt shocks and the deep recession that persisted for the remainder of that decade. However, while the former crisis set the stage for nearly five decades of protectionism and populism in Latin America, the latter prompted the opposite response. Having found out the hard way that the world economy of the late twentieth century was a much different place to do business, a new generation of Latin American politicians and policymakers came to embrace deep market reforms by 1990. In turn, the steep reduction in barriers for trade and finance quickened the region's integration into international markets, where a boom in the flow of goods and capital had long been under way.[1] As a result, the total volume of Latin America's trade doubled through the course of the 1990s, and between 1990 and 1996 leading emerging-market countries like Argentina, Brazil, and Mexico saw a sixfold increase in net capital flows, including portfolio flows (bonds and equities) and foreign direct investment (FDI). This stands in stark contrast to the net negative outflows of capital that the region registered during the 1980s.

Despite this remarkable turnaround, the last decade has also shown that greater international exposure gives rise to more rigorous demands for coherent and credible macroeconomic policies. In short, whereas pre-1982

I

attitudes toward macroeconomic policy in Latin America basically amounted to a strategy of benign neglect, this option was foreclosed by the exigencies of the external sector in the wake of widespread market reforms.[2] Predictably, debates over macroeconomic policy became more politically charged. Decisions concerning trade negotiations or options for regional integration schemes became more contentious, as did efforts to resolve the kinds of currency crises and financial market stress that have intermittently plagued Argentina, Brazil, Mexico, and Venezuela—the four countries considered in this volume—since 1994. As Jeffry Frieden has observed, "increased levels of financial and commercial integration drive monetary policy toward the exchange rate, make the exchange rate more distributionally divisive, and lead to a more politicized context for the making of macroeconomic policy."[3]

This collection of essays examines the rise of a more politicized context for macroeconomic policymaking in Latin America from the standpoint of exchange rate management. Defined here as the price of a country's currency expressed in terms of other currencies or gold, the exchange rate has a direct impact on a wide range of relative prices. Admittedly, all macroeconomic policies are important, but under today's conditions of unprecedented commercial and financial openness in the region, changes in the level and stability of the exchange rate can more readily affect growth, employment, inflation, and other key economic indicators (for example, the relative price of goods, labor, and financial assets). Interestingly, despite a strong consensus regarding the importance of currency policy and the breadth of its impact, little attention has been paid to the role of politics in the choice and sustainability of a given exchange rate regime. Mexico, as the first Latin American country to experience a full-blown exchange rate crisis in the current era of market reform, has been most closely scrutinized. Given the prominent role that politics has been assigned in provoking that crisis, the purpose of this volume is to expand the analysis of exchange rate politics to other countries in the region.[4]

I begin with a fairly simple set of questions. What are the main debates that have surrounded exchange rate policy since the advent of market reforms in Latin America? In comparing economic performance across the four countries considered here, what political economy lessons can be gleaned from the standpoint of exchange rate management? If politics is indeed relevant, what are the main societal factors and institutional mechanisms by which it has been brought to bear on macroeconomic decisionmaking? These questions are briefly explored below.

The Main Debates

Two overlapping themes have characterized the debate over exchange rate policy in Latin America since the widespread implementation of market reforms. The first regards the kind of exchange rate regime that would best complement the new liberal economic model. Opinions differ widely, for the liberal economic paradigm offers no clear guidance.[5] For instance, two Nobel Prize–winning liberal economists, Milton Friedman and Robert Mundell, have argued respectively for a freely floating exchange rate and a rate fixed to the gold standard.[6] Debates about exchange rates have remained a steady feature of the post–Bretton Woods shift from fixed to flexible currency arrangements,[7] but Latin America's overt struggle with these issues in the context of more open economies has revived earlier discussions about policy choice in the region.

The radically changed development strategies of Latin American countries have also given rise to new challenges; a second theme to emerge over the past decade concerns how exchange rate policy can better cope with new pressures. Specifically, the liberalization of the current and capital account has created additional pressures toward exchange rate appreciation. When capital flows accelerate and the exchange rate fails to adjust accordingly, inflationary pressures mount and the real exchange rate will appreciate through higher domestic inflation. Within this scenario, a familiar regional pattern in the 1990s has been the growing tendency toward current account deficits and the increased reliance on portfolio flows and high interest rates to attract additional capital to finance those deficits. The pressure toward currency appreciation under these circumstances has remained steady regardless of the various exchange rate regimes that have been adopted.

The bottom line appears to be a given government's political commitment to implement the domestic policies necessary to sustain the currency at a competitive level.[8] At any rate, as these emerging-market countries have harnessed their economic fate more directly to the external sector through the active promotion of exports and FDI, exchange rate appreciation works to undermine efforts at more successful integration into international markets.[9]

The range of exchange rate options embraced by the leading Latin American economies over the past decade is mapped out in figure 1-1. As the figure shows, there are few alternatives that Latin American policymakers have not tried. The figure corresponds with the three main regimes

Figure 1-1. *Latin American Exchange Rate Regimes*

	Mexico (until 1994)		Mexico (1995–)
Argentina		Venezuela	
	Brazil, Chile (until 1998)		Brazil, Chile (1999–)
Fixed rate	Narrow band (with inner band)	Managed float or average band	Floating rate
Exchange rate anchor	←	→	Monetary anchor

Source: J.P. Morgan, *Latin American Economic Outlook,* August 28, 1998, p. 11.

that Max Corden discusses in his overview chapter: the firmly fixed rate regime, the fixed but adjustable rate regime (FBAR), and the floating rate regime. The left end of this continuum can be characterized as the nominal anchor approach, where a fixed or crawling peg exchange rate is used to exert downward pressure on a country's inflation rate. At the right end of the continuum lies the real targets approach, where the nominal exchange rate is used to achieve such targets as higher employment or a turnaround in the current account. Corden cautions that "no regime has only advantages or disadvantages—trade-offs are always involved. . . . [M]any regimes are possible and can appear successful provided there is no major shock."

Nevertheless, the literature is full of arguments in defense of one strategy over the other. Given Latin America's strong and patently unsuccessful reliance on FBAR regimes throughout most of the post–World War II period, common wisdom in the 1990s has increasingly discounted this intermediate strategy as obsolete.[10] Such intermediate regimes are no longer viable under conditions of high capital mobility and tightly knit patterns of international financial integration, so the argument goes. In other words, countries are faced with the choice of fixed (Argentina) versus floating (Mexico) rates. Yet there are clear exceptions to this notion of a disappearing middle ground, the case of Chile being a main one.

With its longer timeline on liberalization, and its rock-solid macroeconomic fundamentals in the post-1982 period, Chile has been the region's stellar performer for nearly two decades. A main fundamental has been the exchange rate, which until 1998 consisted of a nominal rate system based on a crawling band. Chile's exchange rate band, in conjunction with minimum stay requirements for FDI and nonremunerated reserve requirements for other forms of capital inflows, enabled the economy to withstand external shocks such as Mexico's currency crisis in late 1994. It also formed the linchpin of an economic strategy that sought quite effectively to promote high growth and low inflation through aggressive export expansion.[11] (The Chilean case was not included in this project because it has already been so thoroughly studied.)[12] Suffice it to say here that Chile's main responses to the Asian, Russian, and Brazilian shocks of 1997–98—the shift to a floating rate and the abandonment of capital controls—are testimony not to the discovery of a "better" exchange rate policy, but rather to policymakers' recognition that changing international circumstances warranted a different course of action on the domestic front.

Although the very diversity of options that have been embraced in Latin America under the intermediate banner (for example, crawling pegs, bands, currency baskets) makes it difficult to specify the trade-offs, these stand out more clearly at either end of the continuum in figure 1-1. On the side of fixed exchange rates, the advantages lie in the government's enhanced credibility by way of greater macroeconomic discipline and inflation reduction; the trade-off concerns the extent to which the welfare of the domestic economy comes to depend on trends in the external sector, especially under conditions of high capital mobility and volatile financial flows. As for flexible or floating currencies, the benefits lie in the exchange rate system's ability to adjust for shifts in competitiveness, to absorb real external shocks, and to mitigate both incoming and outgoing capital surges; the risks are a greater susceptibility to erratic exchange rate swings that place stress on the tradable sector, and the temptation for governments to ease up on fiscal and monetary discipline in the absence of a nominal anchor.

Again, these trade-offs make it difficult to argue for the superiority of one regime over another. The shifting policy choices reflected in figure 1-1 suggest that a regime that is deemed appropriate at one point in time may simply not be as viable at a later point. In this collection of case studies we argue that the moment of truth—to adjust or defend the exchange rate—is more than just a technical matter. Rather, it is also a political decision, and one that goes to the heart of a country's commitment to succeed in implementing the policies necessary to sustain the regime that has been chosen.

Macroeconomic Performance and Empirical Realities
in the 1990s

The four countries included in this study were chosen for several reasons. First, as the four largest economies in the region, these cases are roughly similar with regard to their status as emerging-market, or middle-income developing, countries. Moreover, at the very least the term *emerging-market* implies that all four have made considerable headway in the implementation of liberal economic reforms. Although Venezuela's market reform effort was waylaid by domestic politics midway through the 1990s, as Javier Corrales points out in his chapter, policymakers still managed to preserve important institutional mechanisms that helped to rationalize exchange rate policy.

However, despite their similar status, the four cases differ considerably on the dependent variable: choice of exchange rate regime. As figure 1-1 shows, Mexico and Brazil are on relatively new terrain with their flexible exchange rate regimes, while Argentina is on fairly extreme ground with its exchange rate fixed tightly to the U.S. dollar under a currency board. Finally, Venezuela remains in the intermediate range with its exchange rate band. The main departure point for the analyses in this book is this variation in national policy responses, which is ascribed to the kinds of political pressures that affect domestic policymakers.

Just as the choice of an appropriate exchange rate system has elicited differing views, so too has the question of macroeconomic performance under a given currency regime. Chile's success under an intermediate exchange rate policy has drawn the widest consensus,[13] but after agreeing on this, policy analysts have quickly parted ways. From the extensive political economy literature on Latin America, it is possible to find convincing empirical arguments for each end of the exchange rate continuum presented in figure 1-1. For example, in defense of more flexible arrangements, one recent survey of some twenty-five stabilization episodes in the region found that only a third of those based on a nominal exchange rate anchor were successful; the more common outcome was for fixed exchange rates to give way in the face of continued inflation, as opposed to stabilizing prices.[14]

Yet the evidence is ambiguous. Recent studies conducted by researchers at the Inter-American Development Bank (IDB) reassessed the supposed benefits of greater exchange rate flexibility: on all fronts—from the ability to better absorb external shocks to greater ease in adjusting to shifts in competitiveness—a more flexible regime was found to be equally wanting. As the IDB's former chief economist, Ricardo Hausmann, summarized the findings: "Flexible exchange regimes have not permitted a more stabilizing monetary policy and have tended to be more procyclical. Moreover, flexible regimes have resulted in higher real interest rates, smaller financial systems and domestic interest rates that are more sensitive to movements in international rates. Flexible regimes also tend to promote wage indexation. Worse yet, while flexible regimes are billed as a means of maintaining competitiveness, the revealed preference of Latin America is to allow very little exchange rate movement, even in periods of large real shocks such as 1998."[15]

In light of these trends, and in recognition that "fixed exchange rates are never fixed for long," the IDB project explores proposals for dollarization—the ultimate precommitment that a major devaluation will not occur. This volume tackles the question of dollarization only in passing. First, it is still too early in the game to speak definitively about this policy option. Some of the proposals coming from Latin America (Argentina, Ecuador, El Salvador, and several other Central American countries) in the wake of the Brazilian crisis show promise; in the event that they become a reality, the advent of dollarization in Latin America would warrant another collection of essays. But second, it is still not clear if the necessary political constituency exists within the United States to advance dollarization in the Western Hemisphere.

If neither the debates nor the data offer much in the way of lasting "empirical realities," the shift toward greater exchange rate flexibility is indeed an unmistakable trend across the developing world. Whereas pegged rates prevailed in 87 percent of developing countries in 1975, by the mid-1990s this figure had dropped below 50 percent.[16] In Latin America, where this shift has unfolded in two stages, the trend toward flexibility has been more pronounced. In the early stages of adjustment following the 1982 debt shocks, high inflationary pressures and extremely low credibility rendered a fixed or semifixed regime the more sensible choice. Yet as inflation subsided, growth recovered, and fiscal and monetary reforms were implemented, a more flexible system made better sense.[17] Apart from the costs and benefits reviewed earlier, the trend toward more flexible rates has been generally associated with the liberalization of trade and investment in the 1990s, and with the stronger emphasis on market-driven currencies and interest rates.

The data in table 1-1 reflect the macroeconomic trends that have underpinned this shift toward greater exchange rate flexibility in all but the Argentine case. As can be seen from the five-country comparison, by the

Table 1-1. *Comparing Economic Performance: Argentina, Brazil, Chile, Mexico, and Venezuela, 1993–2000*

Indicator	Average 1993–97	1998	1999[a]	2000[b]
Argentina				
Real GDP (percentage change)	4.4	3.9	−3.0	4.0
Consumption[c]	3.0	7.7	−2.8	3.7
Investment[c]	1.8	−3.8	−1.6	1.4
Consumer prices	3.7	0.9	−1.2	0.0
Percent (Dec.–Dec.)	2.6	0.7	−1.8	1.0
Government balance (percent of GDP)	−1.2	−1.8	−2.7	−2.1
Exchange rate (units/U.S.$)	1.00	1.00	1.00	1.00
Merchandise trade balance				
(U.S.$ billions)	−0.9	−3.1	−0.8	−1.5
Exports	20.2	26.4	23.3	26.3
Imports	21.1	29.6	24.1	27.8
Current account balance	−8.3	−14.6	−12.2	−13.5
Percent of GDP	−3.1	−4.9	−4.3	−4.6
International reserves (U.S.$ billions)	21.0	33.2	34.6	36.4
Total external debt (U.S.$ billions)	101.20	141.10	144.60	153.30
Short term[d]	17.6	20.9	21.4	22.4
Total external debt (percent of GDP)	36	45	51	51
Total external debt (percent of exports)[e]	339	357	416	391
Brazil				
Real GDP (percentage change)	4.2	−0.1	0.8	3.7
Consumption[c]	3.7	0.4	−0.8	2.3
Investment[c]	1.7	−0.5	−0.8	0.9
Consumer prices	290	3.2	4.9	7.4
Percent (Dec.–Dec.)	226	1.7	8.9	6.5
Government balance (percent of GDP)	−19.9	−8.1	−9.5	−3.6
Exchange rate (units/U.S.$)	0.82	1.21	1.81	1.90
Merchandise trade balance				
(U.S.$ billions)	1.6	−6.6	−1.2	4.3
Exports	45.9	51.1	48.0	57.6
Imports	44.2	57.7	49.2	53.2
Current account balance	−14.8	−33.6	−24.4	−23.3
Percent of GDP	−2.3	−4.3	−4.4	−3.5
International reserves (U.S.$ billions)	45.3	42.6	36.3	37.3
Total external debt (U.S.$ billions)	195.6	258.6	245.3	241.5
Short term[d]	55.6	38.0	32.0	30.0
Total external debt (percent of GDP)	29	31	45	37
Total external debt (percent of exports)[e]	330	364	406	337

(continued)

Table 1-1. *Comparing Economic Performance: Argentina, Brazil, Chile, Mexico, and Venezuela, 1993–2000 (Continued)*

Indicator	Average 1993–97	1998	1999[a]	2000[b]
Chile				
Real GDP (percentage change)	7.6	3.4	−1.1	7.0
Consumption[c]	5.9	2.7	−1.9	6.1
Investment[c]	5.2	−0.5	−9.2	5.0
Consumer prices	9.2	5.1	3.3	3.9
Percent (Dec.–Dec.)	8.4	4.7	2.3	4.5
Government balance (percent of GDP)	2.1	0.4	−1.5	−0.3
Exchange rate (units/U.S.$)	420	473	530	505
Merchandise trade balance				
(U.S.$ billions)	−0.3	−2.5	1.7	0.6
Exports	13.8	14.8	15.6	18.0
Imports	14.1	17.3	14.0	17.5
Current account balance	−2.7	−4.2	−0.1	−1.5
Percent of GDP	−4.5	−5.7	−0.2	−2.0
International reserves (U.S.$ billions)	13.8	15.7	14.7	15.3
Total external debt (U.S.$ billions)	23.1	33.5	35.0	37.6
Short term[d]	3.1	2.5	2.3	2.6
Total external debt (percent of GDP)	36	42	51	47
Total external debt (percent of exports)[e]	123	152	162	152
Mexico				
Real GDP (percentage change)	2.3	4.8	3.7	5.5
Consumption[c]	0.5	4.1	3.0	3.6
Investment[c]	0.7	1.8	0.3	2.9
Consumer prices	20.8	15.9	16.6	10.9
Percent (Dec.–Dec.)	21.0	18.6	12.3	9.5
Government balance (percent of GDP)	0.0	−1.3	−1.2	−0.8
Exchange rate (units/U.S.$)	6.35	9.91	9.48	9.90
Merchandise trade balance				
(U.S.$ billions)	−3.5	−7.9	−5.4	−11.2
Exports	79.7	117.5	136.7	160.7
Imports	83.3	125.4	142.1	171.8
Current account balance	−12.8	−15.7	−14.0	−20.8
Percent of GDP	−3.5	−3.7	−2.9	−3.6
International reserves (U.S.$ billions)	19.3	31.8	32.4	33.4
Total external debt (U.S.$ billions)	160.3	163.7	162.5	171.5
Short term[d]	45.8	39.9	40.1	40.6
Total external debt (percent of GDP)	43	38	34	29
Total external debt (percent of exports)[e]	162	112	102	91

(continued)

Table 1-1. *Comparing Economic Performance: Argentina, Brazil, Chile, Mexico, and Venezuela, 1993–2000 (Continued)*

Indicator	Average 1993–97	1998	1999[a]	2000[b]
Venezuela				
Real GDP (percentage change)	1.4	–0.1	–7.2	4.2
Consumption[c]	–0.5	0.2	–2.4	4.3
Investment[c]	–0.7	–0.5	–4.6	2.2
Consumer prices	60.5	35.8	23.6	17.8
Percent (Dec.–Dec.)	61.3	29.9	20.0	17.5
Government balance (percent of GDP)	–3.1	–7.0	–3.4	–1.1
Exchange rate (units/U.S.$)	309.2	564.5	648.8	750.0
Merchandise trade balance				
(U.S.$ billions)	8.3	2.7	9.2	10.2
Exports	19.5	17.6	20.9	26.8
Imports	11.1	14.8	11.8	16.6
Current account balance	3.0	–2.6	5.5	4.3
Percent of GDP	4.2	–2.7	5.4	4.0
International reserves (U.S.$ billions)	9.9	11.9	12.3	12.9
Total external debt (U.S.$ billions)	37.8	37.2	35.7	34.6
Short term[d]	5.0	4.0	3.7	3.7
Total external debt (percent of GDP)	54	38	36	33
Total external debt (percent of exports)[e]	167	169	148	115

Source: Morgan Guaranty Trust, "World Financial Markets," April 14, 2000, pp. 55–63.
a. Estimated.
b. Forecast.
c. Contribution to growth of GDP.
d. Debt with original maturity of less than one year.
e. Exports of goods, services, and net transfers.

mid-1990s inflation was finally under control (with the regional average below 9 percent by 1999), growth had been restored to varying degrees, and government finances were much improved in three of the five cases. Thus by mid-decade, Argentina and Mexico had joined Chile in achieving the goals of monetary stability and enhanced credibility that are most associated with a fixed or semifixed rate. At the same time, however, the running deficit in the trade balance and the current account reflects the continued pressure and volatility that these countries face on the external front. The tendency in all five cases has been to linger too long with an appreciated and artificially strong exchange rate, at least until unmanageable external shocks prompted a currency crisis.

This is just what occurred, for example, when Chile's exchange rate crashed under the force of the 1982 debt shocks, the Mexican peso fell in the face of reckless private borrowing and massive capital outflows in 1994, and the Brazilian real buckled in late 1998 under the weight of fiscal mismanagement and contagion from crises erupting in Asia and Russia. In these cases, as in Venezuela, a choice of greater exchange rate flexibility was the immediate outcome of financial crisis. As figure 1-1 shows, only Argentina has held the line in defending a fixed exchange rate in the 1990s, despite its exposure to these same patterns of financial contagion and volatility in international capital flows. Nevertheless, this clear shift toward greater flexibility should not be taken as an indictment against fixed rates: the data continue to confirm that currency misalignments and financial blowups are equally likely under fixed and flexible arrangements. For example, between 1975 and 1996, in a sample of 116 developing country cases where the exchange rate fell at least 25 percent in one year, nearly half of these major adjustments occurred under flexible regimes.[18] At the end of the day, success or failure seems to depend as much on policymakers' tenacity and the ability of political leaders to garner broad support for the chosen strategy as it does on the technicalities of macroeconomic policymaking.

Exchange Rate Politics

This study approaches the question of exchange rate politics from two angles. First, it considers the conflicting pressures that special interests exert on political leaders and policy officials in demanding that the exchange rate be maintained at a certain level. The exchange rate preferences of special interests in the four Latin American countries studied here tend to fall roughly along the following lines.[19] Traditionally, domestic producers in Latin America have been the most vociferous and the most divided in stating their currency preferences. Those producing for export prefer a depreciated but predictable exchange rate policy, while those involved in production for the home market are prone to push for a more flexible monetary policy overall, including an adjustable exchange rate. International investors clearly side with exporting interests in their demands for stable and predictable prices. In the wake of the high inflation rates that prevailed until the 1990s, workers and middle-class consumers have come to prefer overvalued fixed rates, which they associate

Figure 1-2. *Exchange Rate Politics in the 1990s*

	Exchange Rate Regime		
Politics	*Fixed rate*	*Intermediate rate*	*Floating rate*
Elite politics prevail	Mexico (1988–94)		
		Venezuela (entire decade)	
	Argentina (1991–94)		
Greater reliance on societal intermediation	Brazil (1994–98)		Mexico (1995–)
		Chile (until 1998)	Brazil (1999–)
	Argentina (1995–)		Chile (1999–)

with enhanced purchasing power (cheaper domestic credit and ready access to affordable imported goods).

Second, this book considers the broader political coalitions and institutional mechanisms through which monetary policy is mediated. The approach to this second question is portrayed in figure 1-2, which suggests a shift toward increased reliance on societal intermediation over the past decade—through legislatures, business chambers, labor organizations, political parties, and consumers-at-large—in the execution of exchange rate policy. In essence, during the initial phase of market reform in Latin America, policymakers moved swiftly and somewhat autocratically in launching stabilization programs that sought to combat prohibitively high inflation rates through the use of fixed exchange rates. As the goals of a nominal anchor were gradually achieved (price stability and greater credibility) in Argentina, Brazil, and Mexico, along with the completion of crucial first-phase market reforms based on liberalization, privatization, and deregulation, the tasks of economic management changed.

By the mid-1990s, although Venezuela had yet to fully advance on these first-phase reforms, the other three countries faced two kinds of second-phase reform challenges: the need to further deepen market initiatives in areas that lagged (labor market reforms, fiscal modernization at the municipal level), and the need to strengthen the institutional backdrop that supports market reform (more stringent defense of property rights, more authentic regulatory and oversight mechanisms).[20] With regard to exchange rate management, the advent of second-phase reforms meant that the overall economic fundamentals were now sound enough to signal a lasting commitment to low inflation. Despite the heated debates in the literature over where to proceed from here, and the failure thus far to identify a graceful exit strategy from the nominal anchor, some argued convincingly for greater flexibility on the grounds that "after these initial objectives are achieved, and once the fiscal and monetary sides are under control, a switch of anchor will be called for, and a more flexible system—either a managed float or a crawling peg—should be adopted."[21]

But paradoxically, while greater exchange rate flexibility, or the process of allowing the market to determine the relative value of the currency, may imply a hands-off political strategy, just the opposite is true. If anything, politicians and policymakers have been increasingly careful to woo special interests and to offer a wide range of compensatory perks in order to maintain political support over time. This compensatory imperative stems both from the more intense levels of economic competition to which all segments of civil society have been exposed in the era of market reform (and thus the need to offer some respite to the losers in the reform process) and from the inability of flexible rates to fully buffer and absorb the highly volatile external shocks that have occurred in rapid fire beginning with Mexico's 1994 crash.

The four case studies in this volume probe the ways in which domestic politics has tipped the balance in favor of a particular exchange rate regime in the 1990s. Although Mexico and Brazil indeed opted for greater exchange rate flexibility, as one prominent strand of macroeconomic thinking has recommended they should, why did it take a massive financial crisis to wrest an anchored regime from the hands of policymakers in both countries? Conversely, how is it that Argentina has held the line on a fixed rate regime, despite the costs of austerity, deflation, and double-digit unemployment? Finally, why has Venezuela dragged its heels for so long in maintaining a defensive macroeconomic strategy that no one recommends, mainly because of its strong association with the lackluster pre-reform period in Latin America? In all four of the country chapters, the role of special interests, domestic institutions, and old-fashioned statecraft in shaping these diverse responses to similar external contingencies are explored.

In his chapter on Mexico, Tim Kessler attributes the Salinas administration's rigid policy stance to the numerous political-economic contradictions that the ruling party (PRI) had itself cultivated over the course of Salinas's term (1988–94). On the domestic front, the anchoring of the nominal exchange rate in conjunction with an aggressive structural adjustment program helped trigger a long-sought-after economic recovery led by exports and the return of capital flows to Mexico. Moreover, by locating this stabilization-cum-liberalization strategy within a series of ongoing social pacts negotiated between the state, capital, and labor, PRI policy officials were able to project an image of greater public input and accountability.

Hindsight shows, however, that beneath this veneer of *concertación*, the PRI was mainly up to its old tricks of securing political survival regardless of the potentially devastating economic costs. As Kessler argues, the maintenance of an overvalued exchange rate appealed to a broad domestic constituency composed of financial, industrial, and consumer interests. By containing inflation and the cost of mounting dollar-held debts, and by superficially pumping up consumer purchasing power, the prevailing macroeconomic strategy may have been unsustainable in the long run, but it did position the PRI for a political comeback after the beating it took in the 1988 presidential elections. Thus in terms of domestic politics, the refusal to adjust the exchange rate even though the 1993 year-end economic indicators had set red lights flashing can be partially blamed on the electoral cycle and the PRI's determination to prolong its seven decades of control over the Mexican presidency.

But there were also new kinds of pressures on the international front that favored a fixed and overvalued exchange rate. Almost unwittingly, Mexico had become the test case for what David Hale calls the first "post–Cold War surge in securitized capital flows" to the developing countries since before World War I.[22] International and personal investors, who held an unprecedented $34 billion in Mexican equities in 1994, were especially adamant in demanding that the Salinas team hold the line on the exchange rate. Furthermore, Washington viewed the U.S. trade surplus with Mexico in the early 1990s (largely a result of the strong peso) as a main selling point in favor of Mexico's entry into the North American Free Trade Agreement (NAFTA). The PRI used this combination of booming capital flows and the prospect of NAFTA entry, both of which were contingent on Mexico maintaining its macroeconomic status quo, to further bolster its political standing in the 1994 presidential elections.

In the final analysis, despite the tenacity of Mexican policymakers in honoring their exchange rate commitment at home and abroad, the Salinas administration had, in fact, lost control of the macroeconomic fundamentals. Mexico's credibility plummeted as the PRI found itself wedged between the various domestic and international interests that it had so actively courted but could no longer please with a sinking currency. From the standpoint of exchange rate debates, it does appear that the shift to a more flexible regime after 1994 has enabled policymakers to better coordinate macroeconomic policy under much higher levels of trade and financial integration. Yet despite Mexico's impressive economic recovery, under way since 1996, Kessler notes that the PRI has in recent years faced greater levels of political contestation and electoral competition than ever before. This is because of the numerous multiplier effects from the peso crisis—a massive bailout of the domestic banking sector, ongoing allegations of PRI corruption, a relentless wave of urban crime, and an explosion in poverty rates. Ironically, although the PRI has long stalled in the implementation of political reforms that would allow for greater societal intermediation and public accountability, a main legacy of the 1994 crisis has been the ruling party's loss of political control and—as the 2000 presidential victory of National Action Party (PAN) candidate Vicente Fox confirms—the advent of more open politics in Mexico.

Like Mexico, Brazil has landed on a path of exchange rate flexibility through no choice of its own. In both cases, policymakers were overwhelmed by the task of reconciling domestic political demands and international pressures in the context of an anchored exchange rate regime. By early 1999, Brazil's exchange rate was just one of many to come unhinged in the era of post–Cold War securitized capital flows. Thus Brazilian policymakers were certainly more aware than their Mexican counterparts had been of the dire global repercussions of slack macroeconomic policy management. This, unfortunately, did not mean that they were able to exert the necessary political control over economic policymaking. A main difference between the two cases was the more chaotic political backdrop that had prevailed over time in Brazil, where the conflicting and uncontrolled claims of various special interests had fueled high inflation and economic stagnation for more than a decade. This accounts for the cause of Brazil's January 1999 devaluation—chronically high fiscal deficits (see table 1-1)—in contrast to the Mexican crisis, which was triggered by reckless private sector spending and borrowing.

In her chapter on Brazil, Eliana Cardoso begins by asking why policymakers opted in 1994 to target the exchange rate to stabilize inflation when
this strategy had already failed in Mexico. The answer: after a string of
unsuccessful stabilization plans that began in 1986, it was no longer possible to accommodate inflation through the pervasive use of price indexation
and a competitive exchange rate policy. Just as Mexico finally devised the
right combination of anti-inflation policies in 1987, and Argentina in
1991, Brazilian policymakers found their way toward price stability with
the launching of the Real Plan in late 1993. The plan, based on fiscal
adjustment, monetary reform, and the setting of a nominal exchange rate
anchor, fostered an average GDP growth rate of 4 percent from 1994 to
1997 and reduced annual inflation to less than 2 percent by 1998. However, as noted, Brazil's fiscal adjustment never gathered steam, and Cardoso
attributes this to the end of inflation, which made fiscal problems more
transparent but also more difficult to handle.

In terms of exchange rate policy, the coupling of deep market reforms
with a fixed and appreciating currency set the stage for a boom in imports
and durable goods consumption. Domestic demand was further spurred by
several increases in the minimum wage and in government salaries between
1993 and 1995. Exporting interests, long accustomed to a low exchange
rate that favored tradable goods, were not happy with the exchange rate's
antiexport bias. But they were readily compensated by the government's
offering of subsidized credit and tariff increases for the hardest-hit sectors.
Predictably, the government's efforts to juggle these demands within the
confines of the Real Plan were thwarted by volatility in the external sector.
In the absence of the necessary fiscal tightening, the burden of adjustment
fell disproportionately on monetary policy. High interest rates helped to
attract heavy capital inflows, but they also exacerbated the mass of bad
debts that had accumulated within the state banks. By the time the Asian
and Russian crises had unfolded, Brazilian policymakers could no longer
count on high interest rates to attract the magnitude of capital flows
needed to cover the fiscal and trade deficits that had burgeoned under the
Real Plan.

As in Mexico in 1993, in Brazil in 1998 it was clearly time to adjust the
exchange rate. At first glance, the main political constraints were the
upcoming October 1998 presidential elections and the reluctance of
President Fernando Henrique Cardoso to upset his strong prospects for
reelection. In the period following that election, however, when it had

become apparent that there were simply no more substitutes for a sound fiscal policy, the very worst aspects of traditional Brazilian politics again were manifested.[23] Fiscal policy continued to be held hostage to a congress that housed a highly fragmented party system, to regional governors who had long derived political power from their control over state budgets, and to numerous constitutional loopholes that had effectively undermined fiscal reform under the Real Plan. In what had now become a familiar emerging-market scenario, international investors quickly fled Brazil in late 1998, escaping economic indicators that were no longer credible. Brazil's rapid recovery under a flexible currency regime suggests that the macroeconomic fundamentals are back on track; the challenge now lies in the crafting of a viable pro-reform political coalition that can cut through the numerous parochial interests that converged to provoke the 1999 crash.

In the case of Argentina, the shadow of the past and the evolution of political coalitions in the 1990s worked in a direction almost opposite to that of Brazil. From the outside looking in, it is perhaps a toss-up whether Argentina or Brazil was most lacking in credibility by the early 1990s. While the latter had been the slowest to come around to market reforms, both had been plagued by high inflation and extremely poor macroeconomic performance for years. Yet Argentina has steadfastly held to a fixed exchange rate under a currency board since 1991—notwithstanding Corden's observation that "Argentina is not an obvious candidate for a firmly fixed rate regime"—while Brazil has moved to a floating rate.[24] What explains Argentina's relative lack of confidence in its own credibility, and hence its determination to stick with a nominal anchor even after the impressive inroads that have been made with market reform over the course of the past decade?

First, in contrast to Brazil and Mexico, successive Argentine governments never managed to orchestrate a sustained period of "miracle" growth rates after World War II. Moreover, unlike the Brazilians, Argentine policymakers failed to accommodate inflation in ways that at least kept the social peace. The final outburst of hyperinflation between 1989 and 1991 was a last straw of sorts as well as the event that triggered the installation of a currency board under the Convertibility Plan. In the Argentine chapter, I begin by identifying the crucial turning points (the Mexican crash, the Asian and Russian shocks, and Brazil's crisis) at which the currency board could have easily come undone, but did not. In almost textbook fashion,

Argentine officials pursued the tight fiscal and monetary policies that were essential for maintaining the currency board, including a major overhaul of the domestic banking system. While the pressures for exchange rate appreciation and economic volatility have been a continuous challenge in the 1990s, the currency board has clearly succeeded in stabilizing prices and signaling to investors the desired image of a modernized and restructured Argentine economy.

Technicalities aside, perhaps the most compelling lesson from the Argentine exchange rate experiment is the degree to which domestic politics was transformed in the process of maintaining the currency board. The ruling Peronist party, which held the reins of government for the entire decade of the 1990s, had never been known for its modernizing tendencies, but rather for its sectarian and divisive tactics. This all changed with the 1989 election of President Carlos Menem, who acted quickly in renovating the Peronist party and updating its agenda to tackle the formidable reform tasks at hand. Menem moved masterfully in drawing in a new base of constituents that clamored for economic stability, and in neutralizing reform opponents through compensatory perks that did not directly threaten the goals of macroeconomic stabilization or convertibility. Organized labor, historically the backbone of Peronist support, was appeased by the slow pace at which Peronist politicians walked labor reform measures through Congress; exporters hurt by exchange rate appreciation were given lucrative opportunities to shift to services and nontradables in the process of privatizing state assets; and the Peronist-controlled provinces were spared the full force of fiscal adjustment until the tequila shock hit in 1995.

Thus, through wily statecraft, and by bringing technocrats quickly up to speed in sustaining a fixed exchange rate under conditions of high capital mobility, the Menem administration was comparatively successful in reconciling domestic politics with very volatile international trends. The main trade-offs have been at the level of the real economy, where the prolonged effects of exchange rate appreciation have taken a toll on employment and export expansion, in particular. As currency overvaluation has favored services and nontradable goods, the dominance of these less dynamic sectors has detracted from the country's competitiveness and its ability to generate adequate job growth. The imperatives of fiscal restraint have worked against the reduction of business taxes and high nonwage costs for employers. The resulting double-digit unemployment rates and ongoing distributional stress prompted voters to exit the Peronist camp in 1999 and to elect a new coalition of parties that promised to address these shortcomings more aggressively.

Interestingly, any discussion of the currency board became taboo during the numerous electoral contests that took place in the 1990s, as politicians quickly found that to debate the exchange rate was to talk it down. This confirms that, while credible, Argentina's fixed rate is far from infallible. The outgoing Menem team sought to further bolster the peso's credibility by floating proposals for dollarization, which the current Alianza Democrática government has quietly shelved. To sustain the currency board indefinitely, as policymakers say they intend to do, will require faster progress on a range of efficiency-enhancing measures (business tax reductions, further deregulation, competition policy) that can work to adjust relative prices in the absence of an outright devaluation. This has effectively shifted the reform challenges into the microeconomic realm, presenting a set of tasks that will require the cementing of a new political coalition—the earlier grand alliance, which formed around the goals of macroeconomic stabilization, had resisted these very challenges.

Finally, Venezuela is a case in which nearly all of the lessons just reviewed have been inverted. Since domestic politics continued to take precedence over economic policymaking in Venezuela during the 1990s, this is the starting point for the chapter by Javier Corrales. So far, this analysis has shown that exchange rate policy choices were ultimately challenged by domestic politics in Brazil and Mexico; in Argentina, domestic politics rose to the occasion, as the stringent demands of sustaining the currency board required that political coalitions pull together in a more cohesive and constructive manner. In Venezuela, however, a thirty-year-old competitive party system has virtually collapsed under the weight of the country's emergent status as a "reform laggard." To put this another way, the maintenance of a muddling-through exchange rate strategy has triumphed, at least for the time being, over traditional party politics and enabled an elite executive-level coalition to prevail in the setting of a less-than-optimal macroeconomic policy.

What accounts for the ability of Venezuelan policymakers to fend off a devaluation and full-blown Brazilian-style crisis when they were faced with the same volatile contagion from the Asian and Russian disruptions? This question is doubly pertinent, given the 35 percent decline in the price of Venezuelan oil exports that occurred in 1998 and the fact that oil had provided Venezuela with 80 percent of its export revenues and more than

60 percent of its fiscal income in 1997. Corrales argues that the ability of policymakers to defend the country's quasi-fixed exchange rate was due to the nature of central bank–government relations, namely, the emergence of the bank as one of the few modernized state institutions to survive the thwarted market reform program that had been launched by the Carlos Andrés Pérez administration (1989–93). With its autonomous legal status and strong hold over the supply of foreign exchange, the central bank succeeded in using its leverage to stabilize the exchange rate.

Yet Corrales cautions that "although the central bank won the battle, the battlefield was left in shambles." In essence, the country's long-standing political parties were brought down by their own intransigence, and by their resistance to the kinds of market reforms that had now become commonplace in the other emerging-market cases considered here. While Venezuelan leaders have essentially closed ranks and opted for the time being to reject the kinds of market reforms that will be required to reverse the mediocre macroeconomic performance reflected in table 1-1, the experiences of the other three countries suggest that there are no shortcuts to sound political economic recovery in the era of high capital mobility and securitized capital flows.

The following chapters reveal that politicians and policymakers in Latin America are indeed on new political-economic ground. The four cases confirm that, while there may be no single blueprint for the choice of an exchange rate regime, what appears to count most is how governments actually manage their currency policy. Similarly, while the imperatives of sound political management apply across the board, success or failure in the crafting of pro-reform coalitions can come in all shapes and sizes. Mexico, for example, with its strong-willed single ruling party and tight grasp on the various sectors of civil society, appeared at the outset to be a perfect candidate to survive the challenges of its FBAR policy. Argentina's fixed rate experiment, on the other hand, did not look especially promising in 1991, given its Peronist sponsorship and the intensity of past policy failures. Yet the latter's political fortitude and policymakers' tenacity in pursuing the necessary macroeconomic fundamentals worked to reverse these odds. In Brazil, the implementation of deep market reform against a politics-as-usual backdrop drove home the lesson that technical expertise is a necessary, but not entirely sufficient, condition for macroeconomic success. Domestic politics must play its part in ensuring this success, a lesson that Venezuelan leaders seem determined to learn the hard way.

Notes

1. DeAnne Julius, "International Direct Investment: Strengthening the Policy Regime," in Peter B. Kenen, ed., *Managing the World Economy* (Institute for International Economics, 1994), pp. 276–77.

2. On this point, former Panamanian president Nicolás Ardito-Barletta has observed that up until the mid-1970s, most Latin American countries "had very little use for macro-economic policy instruments. Exchange rates were fixed relative to several of the main hard currencies. Import controls were part of the import substitution policies. Reserves were normally kept low and were not built up with favorable movements in the terms of trade. Fiscal policy consisted in deciding how much of the government deficit would be financed domestically because this would determine the increase in the quantity of money and infla-tion. Monetary policy was used mainly to keep interest rates low, producing an excess demand for credit and allowing governments to direct credit to priority sectors, which they defined." See Nicolás Ardito-Barletta, "Managing Development and Transition," in Kenen, ed., *Managing the World Economy,* pp. 183–84.

3. Jeffry A. Frieden, "Exchange Rate Politics: Contemporary Lessons from American History," *Review of International Political Economy,* vol. 1 (1994), p. 87.

4. Good summaries of the political underpinnings of Mexico's 1994 crisis have been written by Peter Smith, "Political Dimensions of the Peso Crisis," Denise Dresser, "Falling from the Tightrope: The Political Economy of the Mexican Crisis," and Jeffry A. Frieden, "The Politics of Exchange Rates," all of which can be found in Sebastian Edwards and Moisés Naím, eds., *Mexico 1994: Anatomy of an Emerging-Market Crash* (Washington: Carnegie Endowment for International Peace, 1997).

5. See Richard J. Sweeney, Clas Wihlborg, and Thomas D. Willett, "Introduction," in Sweeney, Wihlborg, and Willett, eds., *Exchange-Rate Policies for Emerging Market Economies* (Boulder: Westview Press, 1999), p. 2.

6. This debate is summarized in Jeffrey A. Frankel, "Real Exchange-Rate Experience and Proposals for Reform," *American Economic Review,* vol. 86 (1996), pp. 156–57.

7. Fixed exchange rates prevail when governments agree to maintain the value of their currencies at preestablished levels; floating rates allow the market to determine the relative value of currencies.

8. Frieden, "Politics of Exchange Rates," p. 87.

9. Currency appreciation makes tradable goods cheaper in the domestic market but more expensive on international markets, and thus detracts from the goal of achieving com-petitive gains via export-led growth.

10. Jeffrey A. Frankel, *The International Financial Architecture,* Policy Brief #51 (Brookings, June 1999), p. 5.

11. See Sebastian Edwards, "Capital Inflows into Latin America: A Stop-Go Story?" Working Paper 6441 (Cambridge, Mass.: National Bureau of Economic Research, March 1998).

12. See, for example, Barry P. Bosworth, Rudiger Dornbusch, and Raúl Labán, eds., *The Chilean Economy: Policy Lessons and Challenges* (Brookings, 1994).

13. An excellent update on the Chilean experience has been done by Andrés Velasco and Pablo Cabezas, "Alternative Responses to Capital Inflows: A Tale of Two Countries," in

Miles Kahler, ed., *Capital Flows and Financial Crises* (Cornell University Press, 1998), pp. 128–57.

14. Pamela Martin, Jilleen R. Westbrook, and Thomas D. Willett, "Exchange Rate Based Stabilization Policy in Latin America," in Sweeney, Wihlbor, and Willett, eds., *Exchange-Rate Policies for Emerging Market Economies*, pp. 141–63.

15. Ricardo Hausmann, "The Exchange Rate Debate," *Latin American Economic Policies*, vol. 7 (1999), pp. 1–2.

16. Francesco Caramazza and Jahangir Aziz, *Fixed or Flexible? Getting the Exchange Rate Right in the 1990s* (International Monetary Fund, 1998), pp. 2–3.

17. Banco J. P. Morgan S. A., "Making Latin fx Regimes More Flexible," *Latin American Economic Outlook*, August 28, 1998, pp. 11–18.

18. Caramazza and Aziz, *Fixed or Flexible?* p. 5.

19. For a full elaboration of the constellation of special interests vis-à-vis exchange rate policy, see Frieden, "Exchange Rate Politics," pp. 83–86.

20. Manuel Pastor and Carol Wise, "The Politics of Second-Generation Reform," *Journal of Democracy*, vol. 10 (July 1999), pp. 34–48.

21. Sebastian Edwards and Moisés Naím, "Introduction: Anatomy and Lessons of Mexico 1994," in Edwards and Naím, eds., *Mexico 1994*, p. 20.

22. David D. Hale, "The Markets and Mexico: The Supply-Side Story," in Edwards and Naím, eds., *Mexico 1994*, pp. 201–45.

23. See Riordan Roett, "Brazilian Politics at Century's End," in Susan Kaufman Purcell and Riordan Roett, eds. *Brazil under Cardoso* (Boulder: Lynne Rienner, 1997), pp. 19–41.

24. The "classic criteria" for a currency board include small, open economies with flexible labor markets.

2

W. MAX CORDEN

Exchange Rate Regimes and Policies:

An Overview

Latin american countries are notable both for the variety of exchange rate regimes they have chosen or been forced to adopt and for the numerous variations in their exchange rate policies. These features are highlighted in the following chapters, although the discussions cover much more than exchange rate policies and currency crises. In this chapter the aim is to lay out some general principles and to provide an overview of the exchange rate regimes and policies of the four countries included as case studies in this volume: Mexico, Brazil, Argentina, and Venezuela.

Three main types of exchange rate regimes are distinguished here: the fixed but adjustable regime (henceforth FBAR), the firmly fixed rate regime, and the floating rate regime. Although one rarely observes pure versions of these—the reality is more complex and intricate—the classification is helpful. Currently Brazil and Mexico both have floating rate regimes, with some management. In both countries currency crises ended their system of FBARs and precipitated the change to floating rate regimes. Argentina has a (more or less) firmly fixed rate regime, which followed an explosive inflation that ended in hyperinflation. The chaotic exchange rate regime that preceded it is best described as flexible, almost floating, with intermittent episodes of FBAR; however, to describe succinctly the macroeconomic history of Argentina before 1991 is hardly possible. Finally, Venezuela has a FBAR.

Before discussing the three kinds of regimes, this chapter must distinguish between two approaches to exchange rate policy: the *nominal anchor approach* and the *real targets approach*. Each has its advantages and disadvantages. The conflict between them and the difficulty in making a transition from the first to the second have dominated the exchange rate histories of the four countries and, indeed, of many other countries in Latin America. The issues involved here are distinct from those that arise from high international capital mobility and exchange rate speculation, which are also discussed below.

The Nominal Anchor Approach and the Real Targets Approach

The basic idea of the nominal anchor approach is that the nominal exchange rate should anchor the country's inflation rate. The value of the currency is pegged to the currency of another country with a well-established and credible record of low inflation.[1] In the case of Latin America, this currency is obviously the U.S. dollar. If this approach is to work, commitment to a fixed rate to the dollar would mean that low inflation is, in effect, imported from the United States. But does it work? Leaving aside currency speculation for the moment, the effectiveness of this approach hinges on two requirements: there must be monetary discipline and there must be labor market credibility.

If the exchange rate is fixed but the money supply continues to expand, foreign exchange reserves will decline, which cannot go on indefinitely. In particular, the nominal anchor approach means that fiscal deficits cannot be financed by money creation, other than to the extent that an increase in the demand for money allows for some expansion of the money supply without a decline in foreign exchange reserves. Thus the nominal anchor approach will break down if fiscal discipline is not maintained. In many Latin American countries, including three of the four discussed in this book, the achievement of fiscal discipline has been the central problem; failure to maintain such discipline has been the main reason for the breakdown of nominal anchor exchange rate policies. The exception is Mexico, where the 1994 crisis was not caused by a failure of fiscal discipline, but rather originated in a private sector boom.

In addition, if the rate of inflation of tradable goods prices is to be reduced to that of the anchor country, nominal wages must also be adjusted appropriately. If wages increase at a faster rate, real wages—at least in the tradable sectors (the import-competing and export sectors)—will rise, and if they rise faster than productivity growth, growing unemployment and output losses will result. This also cannot go on indefinitely. If the rate of price inflation is not expected to decline because the fixed exchange rate regime is not expected to be sustained, then wage inflation also will not decline, or at least not sufficiently. Because prices of nontradables are likely to rise along with wages, there would be continuous real appreciation. Thus the nominal anchor policy must be credible in the labor market. This credibility depends not only on the exchange rate commitment but also on the credibility of monetary policy. Will monetary policy discipline—usually dependent to a great extent on fiscal discipline—actually be attained?

The nominal anchor approach may not actually involve fixing the exchange rate. There may be a crawling peg. In that case, the rate at which the currency is steadily devalued is predetermined at less than the initial rate of inflation, so that the rate of inflation of tradable goods prices will gradually decline. If wages and prices of nontradables fall at a slower rate, there will be steady real appreciation. At the same time, provided that monetary discipline is achieved, the rate of inflation will indeed decline.

The advantage of this approach is that it can play a crucial role in reducing inflation. It may play, and often has, the key role in stabilization programs in high inflation countries, as in Argentina, Brazil, and Mexico. The disadvantage is that the costs of failure are high—loss of foreign exchange reserves resulting from lack of monetary and fiscal discipline and unemployment and loss of output resulting from real appreciation.

The basic premise of the real targets approach is that the nominal exchange rate is varied to achieve real targets, such as attaining the real exchange rate required for higher employment or improvement of the current account. Implicit in this approach is the idea that a nominal devaluation will also bring about a real devaluation.[2]

If there is some kind of adverse shock—say, a decline in the terms of trade or a reduction in capital inflow—a real depreciation, leading to improved competitiveness, may be required to improve the current account. In the absence of real depreciation, only a reduction in expenditure, one that would bring about a recession and thus a sufficient decline in imports, can achieve the desired improvement. Similarly, when a country suffers continuous real appreciation because it follows the nominal anchor approach but has insufficient labor market credibility, the switch to the real targets approach becomes almost inevitable. The nominal exchange rate will have to depreciate to bring about the desired real exchange rate and thus restore competitiveness. The use of the nominal exchange rate as a policy instrument when improvement in the current account is necessary is standard; for many years it has been at the heart of the balance-of-payments stabilization programs of the International Monetary Fund (IMF). Total expenditure must also decline, of course, so the usual IMF recommendation or condition has been fiscal contraction combined with devaluation.

The Three Regimes: Fixed but Adjustable, Firmly Fixed, and Floating

Latin American history is littered with the corpses of fixed but adjustable exchange rate regimes. In such a regime, the exchange rate is initially fixed, and there is a firm commitment to the rate, but the possibility of a change exists. The country still has an independent monetary policy. However, a change is usually made only reluctantly. The fixed rate period is motivated by the nominal anchor approach, whereas the switch to a more devalued new rate—usually the result of devaluation—is motivated by the real targets approach.

A country with a high rate of inflation may fix the exchange rate as part of a stabilization program designed to reduce inflation, but more commonly the rate is not actually fixed; instead, a crawling peg is introduced, with a predetermined rate of devaluation. At some point there is a devaluation (greater than the rate of crawl) either to offset the real appreciation that has taken place or in response to an adverse shock of some kind—perhaps a decline in the terms of trade or in capital inflow. In other words, the "fundamentals" require devaluation. It is also possible that the required monetary policy restraint was not exercised during the fixed rate period, so that the foreign exchange reserves have been declining. Hence the current account must improve, and again, real devaluation is necessary. The point is that the fixed rate cannot be fully credible because the possibility of devaluation exists. If it becomes evident that the fundamentals are likely to require a real devaluation, a run on the currency will precipitate a foreign exchange crisis.

When there is high international capital mobility and when exchange controls (if any) are not fully effective, the foreign exchange market will anticipate a devaluation necessitated by the fundamentals—that is, by the real targets approach. This may also happen even when effective controls are in place, but leads and lags in payments for imports and exports are also in play. Speculation will thus bring about a crisis even before the foreign exchange reserves have run out, and possibly even before the feared political change or the decline in the terms of trade has actually taken place. The crisis can be set off by very minor developments or even unwise remarks by a finance minister or central bank governor. Nevertheless, it simply anticipates the inevitable, namely, the switch to the real targets approach. Experience in both Latin America and East Asia has also shown that such a crisis may lead to overshooting of the exchange rate—a sharp depreciation followed by some rebound of the rate.

Commonly, governments try to prevent depreciation by raising interest rates, but adverse domestic effects set limits on the sharp and prolonged increase in interest rates that may be required to hold the rate. The market can see that there are limits to increasing interest rates, and thus confidence in the fixed rate will not be maintained. Then the finance minister feels obliged to back up the high interest rate policy with assurances that no devaluation will take place. Finally, the authorities have to devalue the rate or allow it to float. When the devaluation does occur, the government is discredited. Governments, and especially finance ministers, do not enjoy these crises.

The devaluation has to be sufficient to assure the market that there will be no further devaluation. At first, the central bank will sell dollars in exchange for domestic currency in order to hold the rate. Later it will buy dollars back to restore reserves. In this process—selling dollars cheap and buying them dear—it will incur losses, often very large losses, to the benefit of speculators. This is the story of a typical foreign exchange crisis.

The reluctance of governments to devalue even when it is apparent that a devaluation may be required is understandable, as discussed further in the case studies in this book. In short, there is concern that inflationary expectations will be revived, and that nominal wages will quickly rise to offset the real effects of any devaluation. In addition, a devaluation would have adverse effects on various sectors: consumers of imports, domestic producers who depend on imported inputs, and banks and others with dollar-denominated debts. The more fragile the banking system, the greater the reluctance to devalue. Finally, when the devaluation comes, or the rate has to float, the government that built its stabilization program around the assurance of a fixed rate or a preannounced rate of crawl loses credibility. This *syndrome of reluctant exchange rate adjustment* is, indeed, the central problem of FBARs when there is scope for speculation against the currency, and in particular when the country is significantly integrated into the world capital market.[3]

A firmly fixed exchange rate regime may offer a way to avoid these problems. In 1991 Argentina instituted a currency board based on its Convertibility Plan; the adoption of such a regime is now advocated for many countries. The currency board is one version of a firmly fixed rate regime.[4] The idea behind the currency board is that the fixed exchange rate is utterly credible because there is a firm commitment to it, backed by a law that ensures that monetary policy is fully determined by the level of foreign exchange reserves. This means that fiscal deficits cannot be monetized and that the central bank cannot act as a lender of last resort to the banking system. A commitment is made that all domestic high-powered money can be exchanged for foreign currency (for dollars, in the Argentine case). Such a regime should be highly credible both in the labor market and on the foreign exchange market. Hence the kinds of foreign exchange crises that have troubled or destroyed so many FBARs would—one hopes—be avoided, as would continuous real appreciation. It is worth noting, however, that these hopes have not been fully realized in Argentina.

Nonetheless, a fully fixed regime has two great advantages. First, it ensures complete exchange rate stability, at least relative to the "hegemonic" country (the United States in this case), which is a great convenience for trade and capital movements. Second, it ensures that the exchange rate is truly a nominal anchor that disciplines monetary policy and checks inflationary expectations, thus keeping the rate of inflation roughly equal to that of the United States. It is an appropriate approach for two kinds of countries: (1) those with very small, open economies in which nominal exchange rate adjustment is unlikely to lead to real exchange rate changes lasting for a significant period; and (2) those that have a long history of high inflation caused by lack of monetary discipline. Clearly, Argentina is an outstanding example of the latter group.

The disadvantage of the regime is that the use of the real targets approach is ruled out. Without recourse to devaluation, in the event of an adverse shock—whether a decline in the terms of trade, an outflow of capital, or a sharp decline in inflow—the money supply must be allowed to decline (and interest rates to rise), so that domestic demand falls and the current account improves. A recession will result unless domestic nominal wages and nontradable prices decline sufficiently. Any improvement in competitiveness that is needed can be brought about only through flexibility in domestic wages and prices. Labor market flexibility, which is a particular problem for Argentina, is crucial to the success of the firmly fixed exchange rate regime.

Argentina has a history of high and unstable inflation, culminating in hyperinflation in 1989. The adverse effects were evident to every citizen. It is a well-known maxim that things have to get really bad before the people of a country are ready for radical reforms. In Argentina, things got really bad. This no doubt explains the willingness of the government and, now, all major political parties to accept the constraints imposed by the currency board system, which has dramatically ended Argentina's inflation. But another factor was just as important in the establishment and survival of the system. Argentine inflation had been caused, essentially, by the monetization of fiscal deficits. A precondition of the establishment and survival of the system was radical fiscal reform. These reforms are incomplete, as chapter 5 indicates, but those orchestrated by Minister of Finance Domingo Cavallo were indeed radical at the beginning. To some extent, fiscal deficits can be financed by borrowing on domestic and world capital markets, rather than by relying on monetization, but there are limits to debt financing. The market will perceive these limits and will expect the currency board system to break down if a loss of fiscal control is anticipated.

A currency board system cannot be completely credible, because it can be ended. Furthermore, expectations take time to adjust. Although Argentine inflation has declined dramatically from 1991 levels, the decline has been accompanied by considerable real appreciation, with wages rising faster than was desirable if growing unemployment were to be avoided. Furthermore, there has been speculation against the peso, thus causing domestic interest rates to rise well above U.S. rates. In fact, the currency board system might be regarded as an extreme form of the FBAR, with adjustment highly unlikely but not completely ruled out. Only if Argentina fully dollarized—that is, used the U.S. dollar as its currency and unit of account—would there be a firmly fixed exchange rate system. There would be a single, complete conversion of all pesos into dollars, and that would end speculation. There could be no speculation against a nonexistent peso.

A pure floating rate regime is one that has, literally, no exchange rate policy. Monetary policy unconstrained by any exchange rate commitment plays the role that exchange rate policy plays in the FBAR or in the firmly fixed rate regime. A monetary target, or an explicit inflation target, if credible and consistently applied, can anchor the inflation rate, though it may well be a less effective nominal anchor than a credible and very transparent exchange rate commitment. Thus the nominal anchor approach can be practiced through monetary policy. Notably, since 1999 Brazil has followed an explicit monetary policy of inflation targeting. The target is meant to be transparent, providing temporary guidance to gradual reduction of inflation (from 8 percent) over three years and a firm anchor after that. Alternatively, monetary policy can be directed to a real target, such as influencing employment or, for that matter, the real exchange rate.

In practice, floating rate regimes are rarely pure. There is almost always some exchange rate management in the form of direct intervention in the market by the central bank, designed to avoid extreme movements and short-term volatility. The key point is that there is no commitment to a particular rate, and that the exchange rate can be volatile in response to changing expectations. It is fear or dislike of this volatility that has made floating rates unpopular.

Both Brazil and Mexico now have floating rate regimes, but these were hardly chosen. They resulted from crises that left no other alternative. Yet if fiscal and monetary policies are fairly stable and credible and there are no major shocks, floating rates do not inevitably yield great instability. On the other hand, the dollar-yen-euro rates, which do float, have by no means been stable; there have been substantial, longish-term up-and-down movements in the dollar-yen rate that many economists regard as extreme and undesirable.

A variation of the floating rate regime is the flexible peg regime. In this case, the central bank does set a rate, or possibly a rate of crawl, but is very ready to alter it. There is no strong commitment. Hence the crises and other problems created by the FBAR are avoided. Broadly, this has been the Chilean approach in recent years.[5] Such a regime avoids short-term volatility and is a reasonable compromise between FBARs and floating regimes. It comes close to a managed floating regime, because in both cases the central bank intervenes in the market, but there is no strong commitment to a particular exchange rate. An additional and common elaboration has been that the exchange rate floats within a band (or target zone) around the peg, and at the limits of the band there is some commitment to intervention. This variation represents a further compromise between a flexible peg, or even a FBAR, and a floating rate regime.

The Case Studies

The subsequent chapters deal with four countries. Argentina's currency board has already been mentioned above several times. It succeeded in bringing down the inflation rate dramatically, but unemployment has been high because the labor market has not been sufficiently flexible. There have been several deep recessions since 1991. Venezuela, for its part, is a classic case of repeated attempts at (more or less) fixed but adjustable exchange rate regimes designed to reduce inflation, accompanied initially by appropriate fiscal discipline, but followed by a deterioration in such discipline and, finally, by breakdown of the regime as a result of a foreign exchange crisis. This is what Javier Corrales calls the "ax-relax-collapse" syndrome. Then inflation accelerates again and the whole process, with an application of the nominal anchor approach, starts once more. Fuller details of this sad story are given in chapter 6.

For the purposes of this book, the story of Brazil begins with the hyperinflation of 1993. The Real Plan was introduced in 1994, and at its heart was the use of the exchange rate as a nominal anchor. Inflation was brought down remarkably rapidly, and monetary policy was tight, as indicated by high real interest rates. Initially, there was a brief fiscal adjustment, but the fiscal deficit increased again, remaining high. The high interest rates payable on public debt contributed to this increase. All this is described in more detail in chapter 4. The fiscal deficits were financed by issue of debt to the public, not to the central bank. In effect, the fiscal deficit was financed both by domestic private savings and by foreign savings, the latter reflected in a growing current account deficit. The high interest rates, as well as the restoration of confidence in the Brazilian economy, attracted foreign capital inflows. As usual when the nominal anchor approach was used to bring down inflation, there was steady real appreciation.

The Brazilian story differs from our earlier account of a typical FBAR process in an important way: while fiscal deficits continued, they were not monetized, so that inflation did not revive. Rather, the deficits were partly financed by foreign borrowing. Hence the problem was not a revival of inflation or a failure of inflation to decline, but rather the danger that foreign capital inflow would dry up. Indeed, capital inflow continued only because of the high real interest rates, which actually added to the fiscal deficit. An expectation of devaluation developed because of the clear perception that growing (or even steady) fiscal deficits could not be continually financed, which then led to the familiar foreign exchange crisis. The reasons for the reluctance to devalue before such a seemingly inevitable crisis were the familiar ones listed earlier in the discussion of the syndrome of reluctant exchange rate adjustment. In view of the very recent Brazilian history of extreme inflation, as well as a long history of indexation, there was a legitimate fear that any devaluation would reignite inflationary expectations and induce compensatory increases in nominal wages. Not only might this turn the hard-won victory over inflation into defeat once again, but any initial real devaluation resulting from nominal devaluation would quickly be eroded. Here it should be noted that, as it turned out after the crisis in 1999, the fears about the adverse effects of severe depreciation of the exchange rate were not justified by events. Inflation did not reignite.

What the economy required was a severe reduction in the primary (non-interest) fiscal deficit combined with a real devaluation. Had the deficit been severely reduced, expectations of devaluation—and hence a crisis that forced devaluation—might have been avoided. In the absence of devaluation, however, a recession would have resulted. Devaluation was clearly desirable. On the basis of the real targets approach—in fact, the orthodox internal-external-balance analysis—a real devaluation was needed to make the country more competitive and so avoid or moderate a recession that would otherwise have resulted from fiscal contraction.

Conceivably, this view could be modified by the following consideration: the restoration of confidence resulting from fiscal contraction (if it could be achieved) would lower real interest rates and therefore spur an offsetting expansion in private sector demand. Hence a devaluation might not have been required to avoid a recession. Yet it can be argued that such an offsetting expansion in private sector demand might curtail or even offset the much-needed improvement in the current account that fiscal contraction would have engendered.

What distinguishes the Mexican crisis that began in 1994 from the later crisis in Brazil and earlier crises in many other Latin American countries, including Argentina and Mexico itself, is that it arose from a private sector boom, not an excessive fiscal deficit. It is true that the crisis was caused partly by the unwise restructuring of much of the public debt from peso-denominated to short-term dollar-denominated debt (by issue of the now-notorious *tesobonos*). However, although the restructuring provoked an immediate danger of public sector default in 1995, it was not at the heart of the problem. More directly relevant to the issue is Mexico's choice of exchange rate regime in 1994.

The main story of Mexico is simple. Beginning in about 1992, there was, for various reasons, a boom in private capital inflow. This helped to finance a boom in private sector spending, but mostly on consumption rather than investment, which led to continuous and significant real appreciation. Mexico had a FBAR, which had successfully and radically reduced the rate of inflation from its 1988 peak of over 100 percent a year. Real appreciation resulted because the rate of inflation stayed significantly above the U.S. rate. It is important to observe that if the exchange rate had floated during the boom, there would still have been real appreciation, but it would have been brought about by appreciation of the nominal exchange rate. Thus the exchange rate regime cannot be blamed for real appreciation, since that was the inevitable result of high capital inflow.

Also inevitably, but for particular domestic Mexican reasons as well as increases in U.S. interest rates, capital inflow slowed down in 1994, eventually turning into outflow. Given that the domestic spending boom could no longer be financed, there were just three policy alternatives before the foreign exchange crisis at the end of 1994 deprived the authorities of choice.

The exchange rate could have stayed fixed while domestic demand was allowed to decline, partly as a result of monetary contraction, and thus interest rates would have been higher, caused by the nonsterilization of the monetary effects of the decline in foreign exchange reserves. In that case a recession, possibly severe, would have resulted. Besides being politically unattractive, this option would have severely damaged an already fragile banking system.

Alternatively, the exchange rate could have been devalued or allowed to float while some demand contraction also took place; this would have improved the current account and, after a lag, avoided recession. Yet this path was not followed for all the reluctant exchange rate adjustment reasons listed earlier that explain why governments avoid devaluation under a FBAR.

The third alternative was the one chosen, at least by default. The nominal exchange rate was maintained and domestic demand was not allowed to contract. Hence a recession was avoided, at least until the crisis. Foreign exchange reserves steadily declined, and once the market (in this case, above all, the people of Mexico themselves) perceived the high likelihood of devaluation or depreciation, the process culminated in a foreign exchange crisis, leading to a floating rate regime and overshooting of the depreciation.

The conclusion in this case is that, given that massive capital inflow can decline and then turn into outflow, the choice of exchange rate regime becomes crucial. If the rate had been floated at the beginning of 1994, well before the crisis, the slowdown in capital inflow would have caused plenty of instability, but depreciation might have taken place earlier and perhaps not so suddenly. More important, provided that the depreciation turned out to be real and not just nominal—an important proviso—the inevitable recession might have been moderated.

Two Causes of Crises: Fiscal Deficits and Capital Market Instability

In many cases the heart of the problem has been fiscal policy—specifically, the government's inability or unwillingness for political reasons to control it and avoid excessive deficits. This is clearly borne out by the Brazilian and Venezuelan case studies in this book and was true also for Argentina before 1991. Indeed, a study sponsored by the World Bank of the experiences of eighteen developing countries before, during, and after the debt crisis of the 1980s concluded that, with one exception, lack of fiscal discipline was the main cause of the crisis.[6] This study covered the period from the mid-sixties to the early nineties. Although all the countries in that study had FBARs, it is not difficult to show that an overexpansionary fiscal policy would also have created big problems both for currency board regimes and for floating rate regimes. The one exception was Chile, where the 1982 crisis resulted from a private sector boom financed by capital inflow, which came to a sharp end because of real appreciation and adverse external shocks. Of course, the Mexican crisis of 1994, also, was not associated with a significant fiscal problem.

There are actually two channels through which budget deficits can create currency crises. First, the deficits may be financed by monetization, that is, by the sale of government bonds to the central bank. Hence the money supply steadily increases and inflation results. There is no monetary discipline because there is no fiscal discipline. Essentially, the fiscal deficit is financed by the "inflation tax" on holders of money balances and of fixed interest bonds. Given a FBAR, monetary expansion leads to real appreciation, decline in foreign exchange reserves, and the inevitable foreign exchange crisis. As noted earlier, the crisis may come well before the stock of reserves runs out, as residents of the country and operators in the foreign exchange market at home and abroad anticipate the inevitable devaluation. Vivid examples of this kind of story can be found in the history of Argentina during the period covered by the World Bank study mentioned above.

Second, the fiscal deficits may be financed by the sale of bonds in the market. Now there is a possibility of a noninflationary crisis. A switch from monetization to bond financing—borrowing in the domestic and international capital market—can bring about a sharp decline in inflation, with all the welcome by-products this yields. There will be less real appreciation and less decline in foreign exchange reserves. The FBAR can then be sustained for a longer time. Such a switch from monetization to bond financing took place in Brazil during the period described in chapter 4 and also took place in Russia in 1995, in both cases leading to a drastic decline in the rate of inflation. But it only postponed the day of reckoning. With a high fiscal deficit in relation to the growth of the economy, inevitably interest rates will rise, the current account will deteriorate, the higher interest rate will worsen the fiscal deficit even with a fairly constant primary (noninterest) deficit, and the domestic and international debt will build up. The cost of debt service relative to exports and to GDP will steadily grow. Hence the markets will eventually foresee the unsustainability of the situation. A need for rescheduling of debt service, possibly even for default, or, most likely, a shift back to monetization, will be foreseen. As capital inflow to finance the deficit stops, depreciation will become inevitable. Thus the FBAR will break down. Undoubtedly a currency board regime could not survive such a situation either.

If the fiscal deficit cannot be kept within the limits set by the availability at reasonable interest rates of noninflationary financing, monetization is inevitable, as is continuous inflation and a floating exchange rate. If the high deficits continue, the subsequent crisis will take the form not directly of an exchange rate crisis but a crisis of social and economic disruption resulting from inflation and ending in hyperinflation, as in Argentina and Brazil beginning in 1989.

The dangers of excessive fiscal deficits have been widely recognized in Latin America, notably in Argentina, Brazil, and Mexico. The struggle to contain such deficits continues, but it is likely that lessons have been learned and that future crises originating from fiscal policy or the losses of parastatal enterprises will be rarer. Subsequent chapters show that significant victories have been won, in Brazil as recently as 1999. Perhaps, indeed, the fiscal problem will cease to dominate Latin American economic history. Yet in the world of high capital mobility, with liberalized or hard-to-control capital markets, another type of crisis—called a twenty-first-century crisis—is likely to become more and more important. A precursor was the Chilean crisis of 1982. It results from the instability of private capital markets. In this type of crisis, not only the lenders but also the borrowers are in the private sector. The first such crisis, apart from the Chilean precursor, was the Mexican crisis of 1994, fully described in chapter 3. The purest case was the Asian crisis of 1997–98, which affected East Asian countries that had long and impressive histories of fiscal discipline and relatively low inflation.

Capital markets go through stages of euphoria followed by panic. First there is massive capital inflow into a country, and then it suddenly stops and turns into outflow. In the first stage real exchange rates appreciate and in the second stage they need to depreciate. While the FBAR is compatible with real appreciation because of the rise in domestic prices, a failure or reluctance to depreciate is not compatible with the needed real depreciation because of downward rigidity of nominal wages and nontradable prices. In the first stage there is a current account deficit and in the second stage the need is for a current account surplus. The decline in expenditure on domestic goods and services ("absorption") that is required to bring about the switch from current account deficit to surplus is automatically brought about by the private sector panic, usually causing a deep recession. The inevitability of depreciation—caused by the need for real depreciation to moderate the recession and improve the current account—leads to speculative runs on the currency. This happened in Chile in 1982, in Mexico in 1994, and in East Asian countries in 1997. Thus countries are forced from their FBARs.

The policy issues here are extensive. Can the euphoric inflow of capital in the first stage be moderated by capital controls, by avoiding implicit government guarantees to borrowers ("moral hazard"), and by providing more information to markets? And can the sudden panic cessation of inflows and demand for debt repayment be moderated or avoided, also with controls, with better information, and with adequate temporary financial support from the International Monetary Fund? Furthermore, can private lenders be required or encouraged to reschedule their loans at times of crisis? All this and more is the subject of a vast recent literature provoked by the Asian crisis and concerned with the pretentiously entitled "reform of the international financial architecture."[7] The important point to be made here is that such moderation of international capital flow cycles is desirable whatever the exchange rate regime.

These issues are beyond the scope of this analysis, but they need to be noted. They also apply to a limited extent when the cause of the initial capital inflow was not a demand for funds originating in the private sector, but rather a fiscal deficit. If one reflects on the Brazilian case, clearly the fiscal deficit and the debt accumulation were not sustainable. But the sudden turnaround in market confidence and in the willingness of international investors to lend to Brazil was explained not by particular events in Brazil but by contagion from the Russian crisis. In the case of Mexico in 1994, by contrast, domestic political events as well as the growing current account deficit certainly explained the timing of the crisis, even though the severity of the panic—leading to severe recession in Mexico and overshooting of the exchange rate—can only be explained in terms of market fickleness.

What Conclusions for Regime Choice?

No regime has only advantages or disadvantages—trade-offs are always involved.[8] Furthermore, policies that resulted in crises were not necessarily wrong, given the knowledge available to decisionmakers at the time and reasonable expectations. It follows that simple recommendations, such as "all exchange rates should float" or "all developing countries should institute currency boards," must be viewed with skepticism. The most fashionable current view is that, because of high international capital mobility, FBARs are no longer workable or desirable.[9] In this view the choice is between firmly fixed rate systems, such as currency boards or monetary unions, on the one hand, and floating regimes, perhaps with some management, on the other. Jeffrey Frankel calls this "the hypothesis of the vanishing intermediate regime."[10]

One might conclude that all exchange rate regimes are workable when the fundamentals are satisfactory. Problems only manifest themselves in exchange rate behavior; they are not caused by the exchange rate regime. But such a conclusion would be too extreme. Experience, beginning with the breakdown of the Bretton Woods system and followed by many other episodes—notably the East Asian crises and the cases described in this book—suggests that FBARs are particularly prone to crisis. The problem lies in combining a strong commitment to a fixed rate with monetary independence and high capital mobility. This does not mean that the extremes—pure floating and firmly fixed regimes—are the only options.[11] FBARs, in which adjustments are made readily in response to changes in fundamentals and market pressures, can be workable, even if not ideal.

The heart of the FBAR problem is the potential for crises caused by foreign exchange speculation when exchange rate adjustment is reluctant in response to changes in fundamentals, including changes in capital flows. Central banks inevitably make losses when they try in vain to hold to an exchange rate that finally has to depreciate, and finance ministers inevitably lose credibility. But a modified variant of the FBAR regime might still be feasible. Exchange rates must be readily adjusted with automatic adjustment through preannounced crawling pegs when a country's inflation rate rises significantly above that of its trading partners and competitors. Adjustment must not be reluctant. This might be described as a *flexible peg regime*. In addition, there can be a floating rate around the pegged or crawling central rate. Thus an intermediate regime fairly close to managed floating, but not actually a pure floating rate regime, can still be chosen.[12]

Coming now to floating or flexible rate regimes, the evidence so far from Mexico, Brazil, and Chile (and also East Asia) is that managed floating rates, or very flexible pegs, can work quite well—that is, such regimes do not lead to excessive exchange rate instability, other than in the immediate crisis period when the transition to the floating rate regime is being made. In addition, they can be compatible with relatively low inflation, the necessary discipline coming directly from fiscal and monetary policies. As mentioned earlier, in the case of Brazil there is an explicit monetary policy of inflation targeting. But neither the Latin American nor the East Asian countries have yet to experience a private sector boom and bust episode under such a regime. Furthermore, in the case of Mexico and Brazil it is simply too early to be sure that there will not be another episode of loss of fiscal and monetary discipline.

It is also worth noting the Australian experience. The East Asian crisis led to a sharp deterioration in Australia's terms of trade but, thanks to a managed floating rate, the country survived without a significant decline in its growth rate. There was no attempt to raise interest rates to maintain the exchange rate. This experience supports the case for floating, though with some management through direct intervention in the foreign exchange market. A record of conservative monetary and fiscal policies was crucial, as it always will be with floating rate regimes.

Very small and open economies are clear candidates for instituting currency board regimes or for becoming parts of monetary unions. This follows from the theory of optimum currency areas and is a well-established proposition.[13] The interesting and important issue concerns the appropriateness of a nominal anchor fixed exchange rate regime for larger, less open economies. Such countries, notably Brazil, Mexico, and Chile, have made use of their exchange rate as a temporary nominal anchor. If the country has a very high rate of inflation and is willing to embark on a radical stabilization program that includes reform of fiscal policy, there may indeed be a case for using a nominal anchor exchange rate policy as part of the package. Such packages have been strikingly successful in drastically reducing inflation in some cases (notably Brazil after 1991 and Mexico after 1988).

If the country is subject to severe exogenous shocks, however, it will not be suited to a permanently fixed rate regime. Thus it will not be suited to a currency board. The optimal course would be to make a timely transition to a more flexible regime—in other words, to switch from the nominal anchor approach to the real targets approach. If the switch is not made in time, a foreign exchange crisis will force such a transition, as it has in Mexico and Brazil. The problem then is finding an appropriate "exit strategy," meaning a graceful, noncrisis way of exiting from a FBAR to a flexible rate or floating rate regime.[14] Alternatively, the switch in approach could be described as making a faster adjustment within the framework of a FBAR. But such fast and frequent adjustment is easier said than done because of the syndrome of reluctant exchange rate adjustment. Furthermore, if such an exit is expected by the market (that is, if there are "rational expectations"), prior speculation against the nominal anchor rate— speculation that would generate a crisis—may be unavoidable. The best advice is that countries should avoid getting into high inflation situations—usually caused by monetization of fiscal deficits—in the first place, which is a lesson that Latin America is learning. There would then be no need for the exchange rate to act as a temporary nominal anchor.

This leaves the issue of whether a relatively large and not very open economy should choose a currency board regime. Policy analysts will continue to closely follow the Argentine currency board experiment. Obviously, it has some problems—above all, unemployment caused by real appreciation and inflexibility of the labor market. Argentina has also suffered from some adverse exogenous shocks, notably the overspill of the Mexican, East Asian, and Russian crises and the Brazilian devaluation. However, the Argentine macroeconomic record before 1991 was so bad that the nation's commitment to the new regime has not faltered. The fact that the central bank cannot act as lender of last resort for the banking system in case of a banking crisis is less of a problem for Argentina than it would be for many other countries because of the high proportion of banks that are foreign-owned and thus can rely on outside financial support. Argentina is not a small economy and it is not particularly open; nor is its trade as heavily focused on the United States as Mexico's is, for example, and its labor market is not particularly flexible (unlike that of

Hong Kong, another country with a currency board). Hence by the classic criteria of optimum currency area theory, Argentina is not an obvious candidate for a firmly fixed rate regime. The overwhelming criterion here is the need for a nominal anchor because of a history of lack of monetary and fiscal discipline.

The latest proposal in the Latin American exchange rate debate is that countries should "dollarize."[15] Even though the prospect of dollarization has lately become a fad, especially in Argentina, it may still be a sensible option for some countries, especially small ones.[16] Official dollarization—as distinct from private or spontaneous dollarization, which has already happened to a considerable extent in some countries (Argentina and Russia, for example)—is one step beyond a currency board. Hence the relevant comparison is with the currency board option, given that the important advantages and disadvantages of the currency board regime and dollarization are the same.

Dollarization, like joining a monetary union, would completely eliminate the possibility of speculation against the country's own currency, which would no longer exist. It has to be borne in mind, however, that two countries with currency boards, Argentina and Hong Kong, have both suffered from speculation against their exchange rates. With dollarization, interest rates would fall and a significant element of uncertainty for the economy would be reduced. The possibility of devaluation in case of a serious shock—which still exists when there is a currency board—is then also ruled out. Governments lose a residual freedom and thus gain in credibility. That is one familiar trade-off. There is also a loss of seigniorage, which is the interest earned on the foreign exchange reserves that are held as a backing for the money supply in the case of a currency board. Once the decision has been made to completely integrate the economy with the United States, and provided political or symbolic objections are overcome, it could be a serious option for some countries.

To conclude, with regard to exchange rate regimes in Latin America, the future is uncertain. Mexico and Brazil with their floating rates, Chile with its flexible peg and wide floating band regime, and Argentina with its currency board, all seem to be doing reasonably well. Their current well-being suggests that many regimes are possible and may be successful, provided there is no major shock. The most vulnerable are FBARs with their strong but not absolutely inviolate commitments to a fixed rate or a particular rate of crawl. This is how it appears at the current time, in early 2000, though it may not necessarily remain true. But if Argentina prospers while various shocks and capital market instability cause countries with floating rates to suffer, one can expect that currency board regimes, or conceivably even dollarization, will become more widespread.

Notes

1. On the nominal anchor approach, see Michael Bruno, *High Inflation and the Nominal Anchors of an Open Economy,* Essays in International Finance 183 (International Finance Section, Princeton University, 1991); W. Max Corden, "Exchange Rate Policy in Developing Countries," in Richard C. Barth and Chong-Huey Wong, eds., *Approaches to Exchange Rate Policy: Choices for Developing and Transition Economies* (International Monetary Fund, 1994), pp. 65–89; W. Max Corden, *Economic Policy, Exchange Rates, and the International System* (University of Chicago Press, 1994); and Jilleen R. Westbrook and Thomas D. Willett, "Exchange Rates as Nominal Anchors: An Overview of the Issues," in Richard J. Sweeney, Clas Wihlborg, and T. D. Willett, eds., *Exchange-Rate Policies for Emerging Market Economies* (Boulder: Westview Press, 1999), pp. 83–112.

2. On the real targets approach, see Corden, "Exchange Rate Policy in Developing Countries."

3. The disadvantages and unsustainability of FBARs have been most clearly expounded in Maurice Obstfeld and Kenneth Rogoff, "The Mirage of Fixed Exchange Rates," *Journal of Economic Perspectives,* vol. 9 (1995), pp. 73–96. See also Michael Mussa and others, *Exchange Rate Regimes in an Increasingly Integrated World Economy* (International Monetary Fund, 2000).

4. On currency boards, see John Williamson, *What Role for Currency Boards?* Policy Analyses in International Economics 40 (Institute for International Economics, 1996).

5. See Rudiger Dornbusch and Sebastian Edwards, "Exchange Rate Policy and Trade Strategy," in Barry P. Bosworth, Rudiger Dornbusch, and Raúl Labán, eds., *The Chilean Economy: Policy Lessons and Challenges* (Brookings, 1994), pp. 81–115.

6. See Ian M. D. Little, Richard N. Cooper, W. Max Corden, and Sarath Rajapatirana, eds., *Boom, Crisis, and Adjustment: The Macroeconomic Experience of Developing Countries* (Oxford University Press and the World Bank, 1993).

7. For an excellent review of both realistic and unrealistic reform proposals, see Barry Eichengreen, *Towards a New International Financial Architecture* (Institute for International Economics, 1999).

8. For an overview of the issues discussed here, and more, see Mussa and others, *Exchange Rate Regimes.* See also Jeffrey A. Frankel, *No Single Currency Regime Is Right for All Countries or at All Times,* Essays in International Finance 215 (International Finance Section, Princeton University, 1999).

9. See Obstfeld and Rogoff, "The Mirage of Fixed Exchange Rates" and especially Barry Eichengreen, *International Monetary Arrangements for the 21st Century* (Brookings, 1994), the latter being generally regarded as the original source for this line of thought. This view—applied only to the major developed countries' currencies—is also discussed in Corden, *Economic Policy, Exchange Rates, and the International System,* chap. 16.

10. Frankel, *No Single Currency Regime.*

11. For this view, thoroughly expounded, see especially Frankel, *No Single Currency.*

12. John Williamson, *The Crawling Band as an Exchange Rate Regime: Lessons from Chile, Colombia, and Israel* (Institute for International Economics, 1996).

13. The theory of optimum currency areas originated in Robert A. Mundell, "A Theory of Optimum Currency Areas," *American Economic Review,* vol. 51 (1961), pp. 657–65.

14. The exit strategy issue is discussed in Barry Eichengreen, Paul Masson, Miguel Savastano, and Sunil Sharma, *Transition Strategies and Nominal Anchors on the Road to Greater Exchange Rate Flexibility,* Essays in International Finance 213 (International Finance Section, Princeton University, 1999).

15. See Guillermo A. Calvo, "Capital Markets and the Exchange Rate with Special Reference to the Dollarization Debate in Latin America," University of Maryland (www.bsos.umd.edu/econ/ciecalvo.htm [April 2000]); and "The Pros and Cons of Dollarization," in *World Economic Outlook* (International Monetary Fund, April 2000), chap. 1. For a critical discussion see Frankel, *No Single Currency Regime.*

16. In 2000 Ecuador was officially dollarized.

3

TIMOTHY KESSLER

The Mexican Peso Crash:
Causes, Consequences, and Comeback

T HE MEXICAN PESO devaluation of December 1994 was the first in a
series of unanticipated financial collapses that overturned the conven-
tional wisdom on the relationship between market discipline and economic
stability. Mexico was, after all, a model of the Washington Consensus.[1] By
the early 1990s the government had opened up trade, turned a huge fiscal
deficit into a surplus, tamed inflation, and privatized almost all public
enterprises, including the banking system and Telmex, the telephone
monopoly. Although Mexico's success in achieving macroeconomic discipline stood in contrast to its rather sluggish growth, proponents of reform
argued that the foundations of sustainable development had been laid.

The currency meltdown in 1994 and the terrible recession of 1995 led
to a burst of research on what had gone wrong in Mexico. However, in the
wake of devastating devaluations in several of the world's largest emerging
markets, including Russia, South Korea, Indonesia, and Brazil, the Mexican experience is now seen as the harbinger of a new economic phenomenon: the volatility of global capital markets. Yet the behavior of global
investors, though clearly an important part of the story of financial instability in emerging markets, was not the sole cause. Certainly, not all emerging markets experienced abrupt devaluations, while those that did crashed
at different times, to varying degrees, and for different reasons. The

Mexican case demonstrates that the impact of international capital is fundamentally conditioned by domestic politics and policies.

The economics of the peso crash are now well understood. The relationship between the current account deficit and the exchange rate represented a vicious cycle in Mexico's macroeconomic model. At the beginning of the administration of Carlos Salinas de Gortari (1988–94), the Finance Ministry adopted a "crawling peg," a restricted band within which the peso was tied to the dollar and could fluctuate by a tiny amount on a daily basis. Because Mexican inflation rose well ahead of U.S. inflation, the impact of the crawling peg was a gradual but cumulative appreciation of the currency. By 1992, many economists voiced concern over the sustainability of the peg. Because the crawling peg failed to halt the overvaluation of the peso, imports became cheaper and the current account deficit rapidly increased.

To cover the gap, the central bank had to acquire massive amounts of dollars from abroad, which in turn required the state to open the securities market to foreign investors. To retain the confidence of the foreign sector, the peso was kept artificially strong. However, because the overvalued currency attracted more imports, the trade gap grew larger and had to be covered with ever increasing inflows of foreign capital. Even if Mexico had reduced the growth of imports by half between 1994 and 2000 and increased its exports by half, the commercial deficit would still have grown by almost 50 percent, requiring over $100 billion in fresh capital to cover the gap.[2] Any interruption in capital inflows would have rendered the crawling peg unsustainable.

International economic change combined with Mexico's financial vulnerabilities and political instability to provoke rapid and massive capital flight. In 1994 moderate U.S. growth fueled fears of inflation and led the U.S. Federal Reserve to almost double interest rates, from 3 percent to 5.5 percent. As a consequence, the rate of return on virtually all U.S. securities rose, making these highly secure investments far more financially attractive relative to those issued by any developing country, including Mexico. During the same year, investors' perception of Mexican instability grew, following political assassinations and the Chiapas uprising. In the second half of the year, foreign capital inflows dropped by 75 percent. With investments in mature markets now yielding more lucrative profits, global money managers staged a "flight to quality," which put the peso under intense pressure. In a desperate effort to defend the exchange rate, the Salinas administration depleted foreign exchange reserves from a high of $30 billion to just $6 billion by the end of 1994. In December of that year alone, between $4 billion and $6 billion left the country.

On December 20, 1994, just three weeks into the administration of Ernesto Zedillo Ponce de Léon (1994–2000), the Finance Ministry widened the exchange rate band by 15.3 percent. Investors panicked and made a run on the peso. On the following day the peg was abandoned and the peso floated freely against the dollar. The value of the peso immediately plummeted to half its nominal value, plunging Mexico into a surprisingly deep recession.

This chapter offers hypotheses about the maintenance of an increasingly unsustainable exchange rate regime. It then explores the consequences of the peso collapse, assesses Mexico's economic performance since the crisis, and examines the political legacy of the devaluation.

Alternative Explanations of the Exchange Rate Regime

The origin of the peg was persistent high inflation. Despite numerous economic reforms undertaken during the administration of Miguel de la Madrid Hurtado (1982–88)—from steep public expenditure cuts to trade liberalization—the financial authorities could not control prices. Inflation soared to well over 100 percent annually by the mid-1980s. The Mexico City earthquake of 1985 and the oil price cut of 1986 made a shambles of these painful stabilization efforts, prompting the government to orchestrate the first in what would become a long series of "social pacts" between business and labor to contain prices and wages. In July 1987 Carlos Salinas, then budget and planning minister, pronounced the fight against inflation the top priority in economic strategy, unveiling a stabilization plan that replaced the currency float with a fixed peg to put a brake on price-hike expectations.

By the time Salinas became president, the stabilizing effects of the peg had become evident. Inflation was finally being tamed. During Salinas's first month as president, the government relaxed the fixed rate somewhat by establishing the crawling peg. Over the next six years, the administration refused to alter the exchange rate policy, in spite of growing evidence of overvaluation and ever widening trade deficits.

The implicit counterfactual position argued by Salinas's critics was that permitting a mild devaluation before the fateful events of 1994, either by expanding the band or by floating the peso, would have saved Mexico from financial collapse. In the first years of the decade, the peso's overvaluation was moderate, relations with international investors were excellent, and, with high levels of reserves, the government could credibly defend against speculation. With the benefit of hindsight, it seems likely that allowing foreign exchange markets to determine the currency's value during the early 1990s—or even early in 1994—would have resulted in an adjustment rather than a crisis.

Bad Luck and Mistakes

Some apologists for the Salinas team's failure to act in a timely manner argue that the exchange rate policy was right all along, but was simply derailed by unforeseeable events. If political violence and the Federal Reserve interest hike had not come to pass in 1994, a scenario of continued stability and sustained capital inflows is not implausible. Indeed, perhaps Salinas had achieved the macroeconomic stability and investor confidence necessary for a gradual devaluation and a soft landing during the Zedillo *sexenio* (six-year presidential term). Another explanation—one fully compatible with the former—is the incompetence of Zedillo's economic team. Jaime Serra, trade minister under the Salinas administration and then finance minister under President Ernesto Zedillo, was severely criticized (and dismissed) for unnerving investors with clumsy announcements of policy intentions and inconsistent information.

Both explanations have some merit. The events of 1994 were clearly not predictable, and the Zedillo administration's bungling in widening the exchange rate band confused and angered investors. However, it is precisely Mexico's high vulnerability to foreign investor behavior that requires explanation. Foreign capital inflows depended on the continuation of a best-case scenario—historically low U.S. interest rates and less appealing opportunities for investors in other emerging markets. The Salinas administration had made economic stability hostage to events far beyond its control and thus exposed Mexico to the vagaries of international capital flows. Although Salinas's economic team vowed to safeguard the Mexican economy above all else, it ultimately gambled financial stability on the indefinite continuation of a status quo over which the country had virtually no control.

The argument that Zedillo had destroyed six years of Salinas's hard work in less than three weeks—Salinas characterized the crash as "the errors of December"—mistakes cause for effect. Notwithstanding the poorly executed announcement that the exchange rate band would be allowed to slide, it is not clear how the new administration could have defended the peso much longer. With hard currency reserves depleted and foreign capital stampeding out of the country, simple arithmetic suggests that the crawling peg could not continue indefinitely. Moreover, as the peso became more overvalued with each passing moment, the credibility of the government's defense became weaker. The longer the wait, the more serious would be the expected reaction to the peso's adjustment, and the more vulnerable the government would be to accusations of weakness or lack of resolve. If there was an optimal moment to change the exchange rate regime, it was during Salinas's term.

International Pressures

The more compelling explanation for Salinas's resistance to correcting the exchange rate is foreign pressure to maintain the status quo. The most visible source of external influence stemmed from the overwhelming priority the Mexican government had placed on securing Mexico's entry into the North American Free Trade Agreement (NAFTA). Because Mexico's trade deficit with the United States undermined arguments that economic integration would destroy American jobs, the strong peso may have indirectly contributed to support for the treaty in the U.S. Congress.

However, it is difficult to attribute much political salience to something as abstract and technical as Mexico's "crawling peg bandwidth," particularly in the early 1990s when NAFTA negotiations were under way. Few Americans even knew what the peso-dollar exchange rate was or why it was potentially important—especially compared to the more headline-grabbing issues of labor and environmental standards. While loosening the band in 1992 or early 1993 would likely have diminished the U.S. trade surplus with Mexico, it also would have earned the Mexican government praise from leading international economists. In short, the debate in the United States over peso devaluation in 1992 or 1993 would probably have been a political wash. Moreover, the priority of passing NAFTA could not have influenced exchange rate policy in 1994, as the free trade treaty went into effect on the first day of that year.

Another source of international pressure came from capital markets. In the wake of devaluations in East Asia, Russia, and Brazil, there has been increasing recognition of the role played by international capital in precipitating domestic currency crises. The volatility of "hot money"—portfolio capital that can be quickly invested and withdrawn—has been identified as a major constraint on the ability of governments in emerging markets to take any action that might undermine confidence among foreign investors with an extremely short-term horizon.

Although the influence of international capital on national policy is typically generated through anonymous market signals, in the case of Mexico such pressure was quite direct. The Weston Forum, an international consortium of financial institutions, made very large investments in Mexican government securities during the early 1990s. It included some of the world's premier investment enterprises, including Fidelity Investment Company, Soros Fund Management, Salomon Brothers, Nomura Securities, and the Weston Group. In April 1994, following a slide in the peso's value relative to the dollar, the forum met secretly with Guillermo Ortiz, then deputy finance minister, and central bank administrators to offer advice on the direction of Mexican economic policy.

According to a *Wall Street Journal* report, "The suggestions were aggressive." The financiers asked the Mexican officials to refrain from the small daily devaluations permitted under the crawling peg, to agree that the Mexican government would assume losses incurred on exchange rate fluctuations beyond the current band, and to permit them to increase their level of dollar-denominated portfolio investments. Moreover, they suggested that upon adoption of these measures Mexico would receive up to $17 billion in new investments from the consortium and its associates.[3] As journalist Douglas Payne later described it, "In effect, the forum wanted Mexico to further overvalue the peso and assume the risk. . . . [Pressure from Weston Forum] explains in significant part why the Mexican government adopted policies that led to the [peso] meltdown."[4]

Further evidence of global pressure was the rapid restructuring of Mexico's public debt from peso-denominated treasury bills, commonly called *cetes,* to dollar-denominated *tesobonos.* According to then finance minister Pedro Aspe, the creation of the *tesobono* represented the government's "self-binding commitment to fulfill the intended discipline in public finances,"[5] that is, a pledge to investors not to let the currency slide. While the new hedging instrument had received little attention since its creation in 1989, in 1994 the amount of *tesobonos* in circulation suddenly reached almost $30 billion.[6] This dramatic shift in Mexico's public debt structure indicated a loss of confidence among investors in Mexico's currency. Moreover, because *tesobonos* were indexed to dollars, the shift ensured that any devaluation would increase the government's public debt in absolute terms.

Citing overt strong-arm tactics, as well as more subtle pressures exerted by capital markets, some have argued that the international investment community held the Mexican exchange rate hostage. Because the profitability of peso-denominated financial instruments depended directly on currency strength, and because dollar-denominated instruments had to be paid in pesos, Mexican technocrats found themselves caught in a catch-22: they could prevent capital flight only by maintaining an exchange rate policy that was ultimately unsustainable. Clearly, the external economic environment mattered.

Yet the pressure exerted by global investors upon the Mexican government presupposes an already dangerously overvalued exchange rate. The decision to keep the crawling peg, although influenced by foreign investors, was also an outcome of domestic determination to maintain a semifixed exchange rate, which required ever larger inflows of foreign capital. Although the international investment community had clearly gained leverage over Mexican monetary policy by 1994, its power was largely the result of prior decisions taken by an administration whose primary concern was to regain the ruling party's political advantage.

Political Challenges to the Hegemony of the Institutional Revolutionary Party

The root of the Mexican government's adherence to the exchange rate regime was domestic politics. At the end of the 1980s the ruling Institutional Revolutionary Party (PRI) faced its first genuine electoral challenge. Public disgust with corruption, instability, and eroded living standards had taken its toll, and viable opposition parties threatened to win voters on both the right and the left. The 1988 presidential election was the most contested in Mexican history; Salinas's margin of victory, by PRI standards, was quite narrow. Indeed, the PRI was widely accused of using voting fraud to steal the election from the National Democratic Front (FDN), the leftist coalition that later became the Party of the Democratic Revolution (PRD). The leadership of the PRI was convinced that it would have to win votes through better economic performance in order to maintain control of the political system.

Devaluation had damaged the PRI's legitimacy and credibility in the past. Each of the three previous presidents had allowed the peso to collapse. President Luis Echeverría (1970–76) ended his *sexenio* with a major devaluation. President José López Portillo (1976–82), who declared that "the president who devalues is devalued," would regret that he had publicly vowed to defend the peso "like a dog" shortly before he was forced to let the currency collapse at the end of his term. President de la Madrid had been unable to tame triple-digit inflation for most of his term. Mexicans had come to equate a weakening currency not only with high inflation, recession, and government incompetence, but also with national humiliation. With memories of the 1980s still fresh, even a small devaluation, and the inflation it would cause, could be expected to expose the Salinas administration to criticism and renewed accusations of PRI mismanagement.

Linked with pervasive public suspicion of devaluation were diverse domestic constituencies that either explicitly or implicitly favored maintenance of the crawling peg. Large corporations, particularly the financial-industrial *grupos* (conglomerates) upon which Mexico's new outward-oriented growth model depended, had assumed high levels of foreign-denominated debt since the late 1980s. Among the largest fifty-nine economic groups, dollar-denominated debt doubled between 1988 and 1991, reaching over half of total liabilities.[7] Not only were interest rates in global markets lower than domestic rates, but the strong peso essentially subsidized the corporations' ability to borrow abroad. Any devaluation would translate directly into an increase in their debt burden. Moreover, because Mexico's major exporters were also the country's major importers, the natural constituency for devaluation was diluted.[8]

Within the business community, the owners of the newly privatized banks represented a particularly influential constituency favoring a strong peso. The owners, many of whom had made fortunes in the securities market during the 1980s by loaning money to the government and speculating in the stock market, had become Mexico's economic elite. They provided the PRI with both political support for reform and major financial contributions, while the Salinas administration provided them with extensive protection from competition. This small but powerful group made unprecedented profits during the 1990s by borrowing dollars from abroad at international rates and lending pesos at home with huge interest spreads.[9] Any adjustment in the currency regime would have undermined this lucrative arrangement, and weakened one of the PRI's most important and well-established alliances.

Organized labor joined big business in support of the crawling peg, because high inflation had seriously eroded workers' real wages. Wage compression was further exacerbated by the series of social pacts (*pactos*) the PRI had pursued: official agreements negotiated periodically to guarantee macroeconomic stability by obligating the government to fulfill promises concerning spending, taxation, and deficits. In return, labor agreed to refrain from wage demands, and business consented to contain price hikes. Although the unions objected (weakly) to the Salinas administration's liberalization strategy, they agreed entirely with its manipulation of the currency to fight inflation and they strongly supported the exchange rate peg. Through the end of the Salinas administration, the crawling peg provision remained "the most essential element of the *pacto*."[10]

Finally, the middle class, although unorganized, benefited from an overvalued peso that subsidized consumption. One of the greatest benefits the strong peso provided this group was greater purchasing power.[11] Just as the peg made foreign debt cheaper, it also subsidized goods and services such as imported groceries and luxury items, consumer durables, foreign travel, and domestic manufactures made with foreign inputs. Many of these goods had become important cultural symbols of prestige and sophistication. The strong currency thus provided highly valued economic goods to a pivotal group whose electoral support the PRI sought to regain after the dangerous flirtation of Mexican white-collar workers and professionals with opposition parties in 1988.

Understandably, Mexico's opposition parties did nothing to challenge the PRI's exchange rate policy. Although calling for devaluation may have earned praise from some international economists and investors, doing so would have been political suicide. With most Mexicans still complaining after over a decade of recession that their money bought too little, it was an unwise politician who argued that the peso was worth too much.

In sum, diverse and powerful interests made it politically imprudent for the Salinas administration to tamper with an exchange rate regime that had clearly outlived its economic usefulness. The original imposition of the peg was justified on technical grounds—to put a brake on inflation—yet over time that policy generated broad-based constituencies against adjustment, which ultimately undermined the original goal of recovering macroeconomic stability. To these constituencies, a solid currency represented the cornerstone of the new model. Steadily falling inflation and increased buying power were evidence that the model was working. By the final years of Salinas's term, the PRI's own criteria for economic success had been widely accepted by voters who now had real electoral choices. Although it faced growing trade deficits and volatile capital inflows, the Mexican government had very little political room to maneuver on currency policy. While the PRI was able to sell difficult economic reforms as the key to stability and growth, the exchange rate became the indicator upon which the government's economic performance would be judged.

Consequences of Collapse

The December 1994 devaluation had a devastating impact on the economic welfare and financial stability of Mexico. Moreover, it contributed to a fundamental change in the political system and to the end of the hegemony of the PRI. What took most observers by surprise after the float was announced was the extent to which global capital markets rejected the peso. Almost overnight, the value of the Mexican currency was cut in half, and it continued to slide further throughout 1995 (see figure 3-1). Not even the most alarmist calculation of overvaluation conducted before the crash had suggested that the peso was twice as strong as the market would have valued it.

Mexico fell into an economic recession as deep as any it had ever experienced. Unemployment soared, swelling the ranks of the informal economy and putting even more downward pressure on wages across the country's labor markets. In the formal economy, inflation and devaluation eroded real wages. Just three months after the devaluation, the Mexican economy was unrecognizable, with consumption down by half. Automobile sales fell by more than 60 percent between January and February 1995, while restaurant sales sank between 20 and 40 percent. Hospitals and private medical services were down by 40 percent, and luxuries such as international airline tickets plummeted by 75 percent.

One of the most damaging effects of the crisis was the spread of social violence. Mexico City, with a quarter of Mexico's population, experienced an unprecedented crime wave. Robbery and armed assault became common. Taxicabs, which now carried passengers to waiting gunmen, became emblematic of danger. Kidnapping no longer happened only to wealthy corporate executives, but also to middle-class professionals whose families had to sacrifice life savings to pay ransoms.

While poverty and urban decay spread, the most visible consequence of the crash—and the one that changed Mexico's political environment—was the collapse of the financial system. Mexico's banking sector had been inefficient both before and during nationalization. Privatization in 1991 and 1992 increased the amount of capital available to the private sector, but the persistence of high barriers to entry enabled domestic banks to avoid

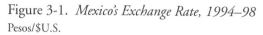
Figure 3-1. *Mexico's Exchange Rate, 1994–98*
Pesos/$U.S.

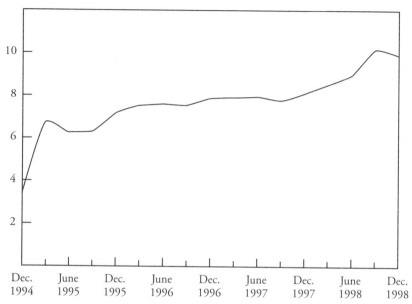

Source: Banco de México, *Indicadores económicos* (1999).

adjusting to market pressures and undermined competitiveness. With the
top three banks allocating two-thirds of all credit, the price of borrowing
money was shockingly high.

Mexican consumers and small business owners were already paying much
higher interest rates before the crash than their counterparts in other countries. Moreover, because the new bankers had no experience with risk analysis and were under pressure to make the highest possible profits on loans,
they lent recklessly. Mortgages and consumer credit were extremely lucrative
sectors, but they also carried the highest risk of default. Even before the
devaluation, the level of nonperforming loans was dangerously high.

As the simmering financial crisis went into a full boil following the
devaluation, the banks contributed to their own demise. In an environment of tremendous uncertainty and volatile inflation, they raised interest
rates from about 18 percent to as much as 120 percent. In the process, they
made loan repayment an irrational act for most borrowers. The banks also
called in many business loans that they had routinely rolled over, pushing
small- and medium-size businesses to the brink and triggering a wave of

bankruptcy. The consumer credit sector melted down into a massive default that paralyzed the financial system. By some estimates, as many as one-third of all Mexican loans were nonperforming by the beginning of 1996. At the same time, antiquated bankruptcy laws and an inefficient judicial system made it virtually impossible to collect collateral from non-paying debtors.

Given the magnitude of the economic crisis, the Mexican populace began to organize independently, express grievances, and press demands. In 1995 a small group of rural debtors called El Barzón exploded onto the national stage, quickly growing into a two-million-member urban move-ment of middle-class and business debtors who refused to pay the banks' usurious rates. The organization offered advice and legal resources, which enabled many debtors to confront and negotiate with the banks. Threat-ening a national moratorium on bank payments that called for more than 50 percent real interest, El Barzón forced the government to address debt relief. Under the motto *debo no niego, pero pago lo justo* ("that I owe I don't deny, but I'll pay what is fair"), the group's militancy, organization, and well-executed publicity campaign earned El Barzón legitimacy among the public and respect as a potent political force among startled officials in the Finance Ministry. The financial collapse allowed what had been a minor social movement located in the countryside to become a genuine threat to the nation's financial stability.

The government responded with a series of debt relief schemes designed to slow the populist momentum for mass default. The basic idea was to restructure consumer and commercial debt by automatically adjusting for inflation and capping the real interest rate. However, because of a poorly executed information campaign, public confusion, and persistent concerns over the calculation of the inflation rate, the government was able to restructure only a fraction of the debt.

Shortly after the devaluation, the banking system was close to collapse. In an effort to stabilize the banking industry, the government began in 1995 to impose tougher capitalization requirements. Because few banks could meet the new standards, the government itself provided the necessary capital, taking possession of bank stock as collateral. Much of the banking system was virtually renationalized. Even though nearly every bank turned to the government for assistance, twelve of them failed outright. Share-holders lost investments totaling about $1.5 billion.

Far more consequential than the capitalization scheme was the govern-ment's assimilation of nonperforming loans. With a third of all loans in default, most banks were in danger of insolvency, raising the prospect of depositor panic and a run on all of the banks, healthy or not. Because the government was in no position to shell out cash, it designed a bailout mechanism that did not require immediate public expenditure. The institution it used to reduce the banks' level of bad debts was the Savings Protection Banking Fund (Fobaproa), a small agency set up during the Salinas administration and patterned roughly on the U.S. Federal Deposit Insurance Corporation. For Fobaproa to take a nonperforming loan off the books, a bank had to agree to write off 25 percent of its value. In exchange, it received a 10 percent zero-coupon bond for 75 percent of the asset's value.[12] Not surprisingly, virtually every bank participated.

Largely ignored by the press and the opposition, Fobaproa assumed billions of dollars of bad debt in a desperate effort to recapitalize the banking system. The small, understaffed agency imposed no legal limits on the amount of deposits it would guarantee. It had limited experience in analyzing bank records and no experience in liquidating bank assets on the open market. By 1998, Fobaproa had accumulated about $65 billion in liabilities, yet experts typically estimated that only about a third of that total would ever be recovered. Mexico's eleven largest banks accounted for about half of Fobaproa's liabilities. Because they had to pay a quarter of losses, they were exposed to a loss of over $5 billion. Worse still, they could lose billions more on bad loans not covered by Fobaproa. These figures rivaled the banks' total net worth.

Political Fallout of the Bank Rescue

In April 1998 President Zedillo sent Congress a package of banking reforms to guide Mexico out of its financial wilderness. While some regulatory issues prompted grumbling among the opposition,[13] the central provision—the incorporation of Fobaproa liabilities into formal public sector debt—sparked a firestorm in Congress. The government argued that the measure was needed to strengthen the banking system and protect innocent savers who held their deposits at troubled banks. Conferring public debt status on Fobaproa obligations would ensure depositor confidence and enable the government to restructure its obligations through standard financial instruments and spread out the fiscal burden over time.

The financial scope of the bailout was breathtaking. Fobaproa's $65 billion portfolio approached 15 percent of Mexico's gross domestic product (GDP), an amount equal to almost one-third of the banking system's total assets and far more than the banks' total capital. The proposal represented the largest increase in the internal debt in Mexico's history, from about 28 percent of GDP to 42 percent.

The two main opposition parties, the Party of the Democratic Revolution and the National Action Party (PAN), accused the PRI of underwriting the debts of its wealthy and corrupt allies with taxpayers' money. Widespread disgust over yet another economic crisis cost the PRI its longstanding control of Congress—in July 1997 the PRD and PAN together won a majority in the lower house. The executive branch would no longer enjoy rubber-stamped approval of its policy initiatives. Following these watershed midterm elections, the approval of Zedillo's bank rescue package became the center of the struggle for political power in Mexico.

Government officials admonished Congress not to play politics with the country's economic well-being. Finance Undersecretary Martin Werner declared that legislators had the choice between "governing for the future or settling old scores."[14] In April 1998, claiming that financial collapse could be prevented only through prompt legislative action, President Zedillo asked Congress to hold a special session in August to approve the bailout package. Not only did the lower house refuse, it redoubled its efforts to discredit the proposal.

Zedillo's bank rescue scheme temporarily united the ideologically divided opposition parties, which used three arguments to attack the bailout. First, both the PAN and the PRD maintained that the recapitalization of the banks violated the constitution. Indeed, they claimed that then finance minister Guillermo Ortiz and Banco de México governor Miguel Mancera had acted illegally in rescuing the banks, because Fobaproa's liabilities were never authorized by Congress.[15] As PAN representative Carlos Plascencia stated, "Fobaproa isn't a matter of yes or no; this proposal only offends us because it's about an aspect of legality, not negotiation."[16]

Second, the opposition argued that Fobaproa had bankrupted the country through incompetence and mismanagement. Because it failed to obtain basic loan information such as debtors' credit history, the untested agency found it extremely difficult to liquidate risky assets for even a fraction of their face value. Moreover, because it quickly took on vast numbers of loans with minimal analysis, it was accused of fostering moral hazard among businesses that saw an easy opportunity to unload their debt onto taxpayers.

Finally, the most politically explosive accusations concerned favoritism. Although Fobaproa technically was a deposit protection plan, its most immediate effect was to benefit many of Mexico's wealthy and unscrupulous entrepreneurs. Opposition politicians, relying on the banks' own financial data and the testimony of known financial criminals, exposed what appeared to be sweet deals offered to some of the country's wealthiest businessmen and longtime contributors to the PRI.

For the first time in its history, Congress became a tool of investigation, providing evidence indicating that rich and well-connected businessmen had turned to Fobaproa to erase huge financial obligations. Opposition politicians declared in July 1998 that they had obtained Fobaproa documents suggesting that just 604 loans made to some of Mexico's wealthiest entrepreneurs represented almost half of the agency's total liabilities—almost certainly an exaggeration, but politically effective. A week later, in spite of government protests about bank secrecy laws, the PRD revealed a list of names of the top 310 businesses and people whose defaulted loans had been assimilated by Fobaproa. Among those names were notorious financial criminals and several major Mexican corporations.

The Bailout Deal and the Advent of Mexican Party Politics

For most of the century, the PRI was the exclusive arena for negotiation among diverse economic interests. The stubborn maintenance of an increasingly unviable exchange rate regime under President Salinas, while influenced by the rise of powerful opposition parties, reflected the persistence of the PRI's policymaking hegemony. In an effort to recover the support of the PRI's traditional constituencies, the party's leadership—and it alone—conceived, implemented, and maintained the crawling peg. In contrast, the politics and policy outcomes of the banking bailout under President Zedillo were driven by viable and robust opposition parties.

The trend toward more authentic multiparty competition gradually increased after the peso collapse, particularly during the debate over Fobaproa. As the dominant party with the broadest social base, the PRI steered away from ideology and portrayed itself as a pragmatic party willing to address the threat of financial collapse with substantive policy proposals. However, burdened with blame for the crisis, it also adopted a flexible and conciliatory posture to minimize further political damage. As the voice of economic sobriety, the center-right PAN found itself in a difficult position. On the one hand, its core small business constituency demanded timely resolution of the financial crisis; on the other hand, any cooperation with the PRI could easily be portrayed by the left as a sellout, which would undermine the PAN's ability to broaden its appeal among popular sectors.

Meanwhile, the PRD nurtured its own image as the sole protector of Mexican social justice. Its leadership realized that cooperation between the other two parties would eventually lead to a political compromise over the financial package, and it positioned itself to expose any legislative deal as a betrayal of public trust. As political analyst Luis Rubio explained, the "PAN recognizes the need to approve the government's debt increase bill, but does not want to pay a hefty political price for doing so. PRD has stolen the legislative agenda from the other parties and is doing everything it can to enhance the political cost of the whole deal."[17] Characterizing the congressional talks as a sham, the PRD publicly announced its exit from the ongoing negotiations in the fall of 1998 and dedicated itself to attacking any progress toward a resolution as undemocratic and unconstitutional.

As expected, after months of politically motivated acrimony, the PAN began to cooperate with the PRI in crafting an alternative proposal to Zedillo's much-maligned financial reform package. The initiative included several provisions designed to provide political cover for members of Congress seeking to end legislative brinkmanship. First, it denied coverage of loans over five million pesos and included smaller credit card and mortgage obligations in Fobaproa. The compromise helped deflect public criticism by making the banks responsible for the largest business debts, which carried lower administrative costs; this would ostensibly enable the banks to increase collection rates. Second, the new package provided aid for smaller debtors who had continued servicing their loans throughout the crisis, specifically targeting small- and medium-size businesses, farmers, and homeowners. The political value of these constituencies—the urban middle class and rural landowners—facilitated the compromise between the PAN and the PRI.

Finally, the legislation incorporated the PAN demand to eliminate Fobaproa and relocate its portfolio to a new agency, the Bank Deposit Insurance Institute (IPAB). Through a series of legal maneuvers, IPAB would not officially transfer its obligations to the public debt. However, as critics immediately pointed out, because IPAB's obligations would be financed from a special allocation of the federal budget, the change amounted to nothing more than a legal fiction that fulfilled the spirit, if not the letter, of Zedillo's original proposal. The provision also prohibited any public officials who had participated in the 1995 bailout from serving on IPAB's board of directors. Although the PAN had given up its longtime demand for former finance minister Guillermo Ortiz's resignation, at least it could claim that it had prevented the unpopular central banker from meddling further with the bank rescue.

On December 12, 1998, the PAN and the PRI overwhelmingly approved the reform package.[18] Although the long-term budget implications of the bailout remained disturbing, both the PAN and the PRI publicly congratulated themselves for rising above politics and saving the country's economy. PRD members were incensed, calling the Congress "traitors to the fatherland" and characterizing legislators on the right as "*panista* whores."[19] Protesters from El Barzón muscled their way onto the legislative floor and pelted PAN and PRI members with flour and tomatoes. The PRD had reveled in its role as political spoiler, but it also gave the other two parties the opportunity to isolate it from the moderate, mainstream electorate. Both the PRI and the PAN characterized the PRD as a force that, given real power, would destroy the financial system to gain political advantage.

The Fobaproa deal kept banking at the center of the political stage in Mexico. In July 1999 a long-awaited foreign audit of the bank rescue commissioned by Congress was completed. The $20 million audit, led by Canadian Michael Mackey, concluded that the crisis resulted from significant shortcomings in the bank reprivatization process, inadequate experience among the new owners, and poor regulation by government authorities. Given that these problems arose during the Salinas *sexenio,* this finding served the Zedillo administration well. However, the audit report also concluded that pumping money into insolvent banks had cost Mexican taxpayers far more than simply allowing the banks to fail would have. The opposition focused on the finding that $8 billion worth of the loans were of questionable legality, $638 million were clearly illegal, and $4.4 billion involved loans to directly affiliated companies. However, Mackey's report failed to uncover evidence that any government official had broken the law. Disappointed critics charged that the government had used the bank secrecy law to deny the audit team access to information necessary to prove specific cases of criminality.[20]

Evaluating the Crisis: How Effective Was Reform?

The debate over what the Mexican devaluation and its aftermath teach us about economic policy reform is highly polarized. Mexico was a genuinely reformist emerging market whose financial collapse took both critics and supporters of liberalization by surprise. While the former portrayed the crisis as the inevitable outcome of unrestricted markets, the latter argued that Mexico's firm foundation of reforms saved the country from what otherwise would have been a lengthy depression.

For critics of economic liberalization, the Mexican devaluation and subsequent recession offered evidence that free markets lead developing countries to crisis, not growth. If any of the so-called emerging markets were to succeed by following the Washington Consensus, Mexico should have been the one to do it. The government was genuinely committed to reform, and its financial authorities were among the world's most technically capable, having received doctorates in the economics departments of elite U.S. universities. Yet even with these advantages, which few other developing countries could match, the government implemented incongruent and unsustainable policies that destroyed the gains achieved through fiscal discipline.

Moreover, continues the critique, liberalization failed to save ninety million Mexicans from a devastating recession—and the resulting decay of the social fabric—despite the unique benefits of close integration with the world's largest economy. The Clinton administration orchestrated a $50 billion bailout with the International Monetary Fund that injected liquidity into the reeling economy. A booming U.S. economy then absorbed massive increases in Mexican exports. As expected, the Mexican deficit with the United States quickly turned to a large surplus (see figure 3-2). Yet the average Mexican received little benefit from the improved macroeconomic performance. Even with a devalued currency that made Mexican goods extremely competitive, the economy failed to generate enough growth or jobs to shield millions from deepening poverty. By the mid-1990s, real per capita income had still not recovered to 1981 levels.

Finally, according to trade unions, protectionist legislators, and pundits in the United States, the Mexican crisis destroyed American jobs even as it undermined Mexican living standards. Following the devaluation, the weakened peso made Mexican goods extremely competitive in U.S. markets. NAFTA, it was argued, had been a Trojan horse. Free traders had brought a seemingly healthy and robust developing nation directly into the U.S. market by promising that continued growth meant ever expanding employment in the high-wage export sector. However, in less than a

Figure 3-2. *Mexico's Current Account Deficit, 1988–97*
U.S. $ millions

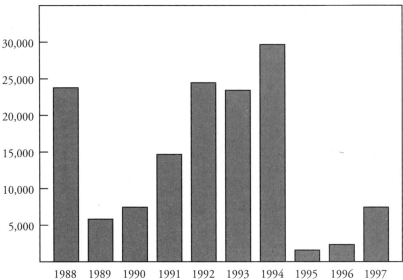

Source: Banco de México, *Indicadores económicos* (1999).

year the peso devaluation turned American consumers into the lifeline of
Mexico's economy, which clung to survival only by exporting massive
amounts of goods to its thriving northern neighbor.

The assertion that Mexico suffered deeply as a result of the devaluation
is indisputable. However, the argument that Mexico's economic liberalization caused the peso crash conflates specific policy errors with general economic reform. The financial collapse was not the result of trade and
investment liberalization or fiscal streamlining. Rather, the rapid and
unregulated opening of capital markets and the banking sector, combined
with an unsustainable exchange rate policy, were the main factors behind
the crisis.

Proponents of liberalization maintain—with considerable evidence—
that structural reform and openness enabled the Mexican economy to
recover from policy mistakes and exogenous shocks much more rapidly
than it could have under previous inward-oriented policies. Since the
exchange rate began to float, outward-oriented growth has proven quite

Figure 3-3. *Mexico's GDP Growth, 1994–98*
Percent

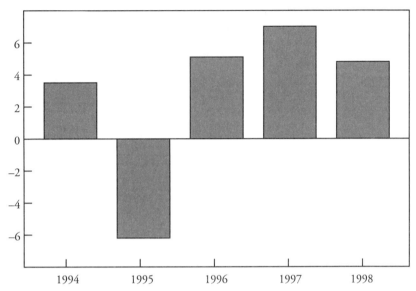

Source: Banco de México, *Indicadores económicos* (1999).

viable and dynamic. Although the recession following the devaluation was arguably the deepest of the century, fiscal discipline and an open business climate that welcomed foreign investment helped Mexico turn a 6.2 percent decline in GDP in 1995 into robust growth over the next three years (see figure 3-3). By contrast, the devaluation of 1982 had plunged Mexico into a decade of inflation and stagnation.

The main reason for the recovery, of course, was increased trade with the United States. But just as important as the expansion of Mexican exports was their composition. Largely as a result of reduced barriers to foreign investment, Mexico is no longer simply an assembly platform for imported inputs. Mexicans are increasingly participating in high value added activities of production and distribution, such as research and development, engineering, and marketing, for both foreign and domestic markets. Traditional maquiladoras are still a major presence in export activities, but far more professional and technical employment is now being generated south of the Rio Grande. Moreover, Mexico's industrial expansion is no longer concentrated exclusively in the border region.[21]

Even more impressive, Mexico achieved these results despite severe exogenous shocks. The drop in international oil prices forced the government to slash the budget three times in 1998 and reduced foreign exchange earnings, while the financial collapse of East Asia and Russia caused global investors to shun emerging markets indiscriminately. Mexico's ability to continue growing in spite of reduced public spending and foreign capital inflows stood in contrast to the experiences of other emerging markets facing similar constraints. That performance reflected the effectiveness of fundamental reforms in fiscal management, trade, and investment.

As for regional impact, far from harming the U.S. economy, reform in Mexico helped shield its neighbor from economic shocks generally associated with the devaluation of a major trading partner. Evidence of any economic drag was scarce. In the years following the crisis, economic expansion in the United States actually accelerated. As its GDP galloped ahead of that of virtually all developed countries, U.S. inflation remained negligible—in contrast with that of Mexico (see figure 3-4)—unemployment dropped to its lowest level in thirty years, the stock market skyrocketed, and the federal government began racking up huge fiscal surpluses. And although Mexico did generate a large trade surplus with the United States, the actual level of U.S. exports to Mexico, and the jobs associated with it, varied little. Once again, a comparison is illuminating. Whereas Mexico imported $24 billion in goods in 1981, it imported goods worth only $9 billion in 1983 and took seven more years to reach predebt crisis import levels; after the 1994 devaluation, however, with low tariffs embedded in the NAFTA agreement, Mexico took only eighteen months to recover its precrisis import levels. By exporting more goods to the U.S. market, Mexico did not take American jobs, but simply displaced goods previously exported by other emerging markets.

Mexico's economic transformation has not eliminated pervasive poverty and long-standing social inequality, and the "dual economy" is more evident now than ever. Millions of citizens are not even integrated into the domestic economy, much less into global export markets. Yet the argument against liberalization is based on the implausible assertion that employment and wages would somehow be better without reform. Although exports alone will not lift millions of peasants and underemployed people out of poverty, Mexico's integration into markets for traditional and sophisticated goods is essential for generating quality jobs, which in turn creates demand for both basic and higher education. Economic opening has not been a panacea for Mexican development, but it dramatically shortened

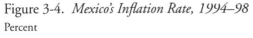

Figure 3-4. *Mexico's Inflation Rate, 1994–98*
Percent

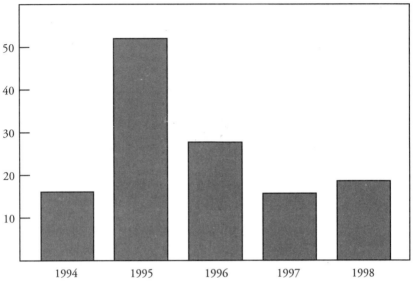

Source: Banco de México, *Indicadores económicos* (1999).

what could have been another lost decade of crisis, and it has provided the macroeconomic discipline and trade opportunities upon which future growth will ultimately depend.

Beyond Reform: Mexico's Development Challenge

The achievements of Mexico's export sector, though significant, will not be sufficient to generate sustained or broad-based economic growth. Most fundamentally, Mexico lacks a viable banking sector. While virtually every other major economic sector has recovered since the 1994 devaluation, the financial system remains mired in crisis and incapable of providing credit for productive investment.[22] Foreign capital has made considerable investment possible since the peso crash, but it will not be a substitute for home-grown development.

Only Mexico's largest corporations have regular access to bank capital.[23] Still lacking risk-analysis capabilities and desperate to avoid further bad loans, banks shun lending to smaller businesses or individuals. Even major companies with sufficient capital to expand are being undermined by the continued domestic credit crunch. According to Ignacio Toussaint, chief financial officer of Mexico's second largest retailer, Grupo Gigante, "The impact is indirect through our customers and suppliers. If they can't fund purchases or reinvest in their businesses, they won't grow with us."[24] Even for those who can get credit, interest rates remain prohibitive. In May 1999, while Mexican banks paid an average of 10 percent on long-term deposits, they charged 37 percent on auto loans and 55 percent on credit cards, one of the highest spreads in the world.[25]

Notwithstanding the enormous obligations assumed by Fobaproa, Mexican banks are still fragile institutions. IPAB head Vicente Corta won praise for tough actions, such as taking over and auctioning off the assets of financially insolvent Banca Serfín, Mexico's third largest bank. Given that the bank was controlled by Adrián Sada, a powerful and politically connected industrialist, IPAB's insistence that the owners lose 100 percent of their investment earned it respect even among opposition politicians.[26] However, the weakness of the banking system is pervasive. In June 1999 Moody's Investors Service reported that Mexican banks were still over $13 billion away from adequate capitalization.[27] Of the seventy-four countries for which Moody's evaluates bank system stability, Mexico ranked the ninth worst, below Kazakstan, Romania, and Tunisia.[28]

Mexico's private sector has recognized that the country's crippled banking system limits opportunities for growth. The prospect of a prolonged credit crunch has prompted ideas that would have been unthinkable just a few years ago. In early 1999 some of the most influential entrepreneurs in the country proposed the formal dollarization of the economy—a plan already articulated by the governments of Argentina and Ecuador.[29] Eugenio Clariond, president of the elite Council of Mexican Businessmen (CMHN), publicly asked President Zedillo to endorse a plan to enable Mexican firms to conduct basic transactions in dollars. He went on to explain that the resulting benefits of low inflation, growth, and low interest rates would lay the foundation for eventual monetary union with Mexico's NAFTA partners. Zedillo emphatically rejected the idea, maintaining that the most effective instrument for reducing financial volatility was the floating exchange rate.[30] Cautious government financial authorities are unlikely to accept the risk of dollarization in the near future, but the fact that the CMHN, the Mexican Bankers' Association, and the country's largest industrial chamber took the proposition seriously suggests that

Mexico's private sector is deeply worried about the country's current potential for development.

The logic behind dollarization is to deepen Mexico's integration with the U.S. economy, a strategy that paid off well during the latter's remarkable economic boom of the 1990s. However, Mexico's heavy dependence on the U.S. market—the destination of over 80 percent of Mexico's $115 billion in exports in 1998—will have severe consequences if its northern neighbor falls into recession, and herein lies the risk of dollarization for Mexico.

The Mexican government is acutely aware of the need to diversify its export markets. The current account deficit, virtually eliminated following the devaluation, crept back to over $7 billion by 1997 and has continued to rise. Although Mexico sells more than ever before, its stubborn trade gap suggests a structural dependence on imports that could once again jeopardize macroeconomic stability. In 1999, Mexico concluded negotiations on free trade agreements with the European Union (which purchased only $4 billion of Mexican goods in 1998) and Israel. Both became effective on July 1, 2000. In addition, in 2000 Mexico established trade agreements with Guatemala, Honduras, and El Salvador as a bloc. Those agreements will create important opportunities for Mexican producers, but their effects will still be minuscule compared to NAFTA. For better or for worse, Mexican growth will be closely linked to the health of the U.S. economy for the foreseeable future.

Conclusion: The Political Legacy of the Crisis

In light of Mexico's turnaround, one lasting consequence of the currency crisis is likely to be policy continuity and the gradual deepening of structural reform. Even though Mexico's main architects of liberalization, Salinas, Serra, and Ortiz, have been blamed for the collapse, the original economic project lives on. Not even the most outspoken PRD politician calls for a return to import substitution, protectionism, or state ownership of production.

The main debates over the proper role of the government concern corruption, administrative and regulatory competence, and basic issues of social protection and redistribution. Populism is far from dead in Mexican politics, but it will not reverse the fundamental transformations in Mexican trade and investment. Even the budget process, which is subject to more domestic political pressure than economic policies that affect foreign capital or market access, is likely to remain disciplined no matter which party is in office.

Widespread opposition to the return of PRI paternalism—as evidenced by the dramatic victory of PAN candidate Vicente Fox in the July 2000 presidential election—indicates an even deeper transformation of the Mexican state. Indeed, the most enduring consequence of the crisis was the opening of the political process itself. Although the peso devaluation of 1994 was not the direct cause of Mexico's political liberalization or Fox's victory, it did enable opposition parties to exploit opportunities for political opening as never before. It not only accelerated the process of democratization but also shaped the nature of political competition and the legislative process in a country that, in living memory, had been ruled by a single party.

That was not supposed to happen. Salinas's reform project, which accelerated the process begun under President de la Madrid, was based on a clear sequencing strategy. Like the Communist Party of China—and unlike that of the former Soviet Union—the PRI restructured the economy before opening up the political system to real competition. During this critical period, the party's control of the main social organizations allowed it to minimize popular mobilization against reform.

History suggests that the PRI's strategy was well founded. When Salinas won the 1988 elections, the remarkable electoral strength of the left and popular outrage over vote-counting irregularities put the PRI on notice that it would no longer be able to ensure control of the presidency with fraud. Six years later, the recovery of economic stability and the apparent boost in living standards—largely the result of an unsustainable exchange rate policy—had convinced the electorate to stay with the PRI. Ernesto Zedillo won the presidency in 1994 in a relatively clean election.

The shock of the peso crash coincided with the rise of well-organized and professional opposition parties that gave voters real political alternatives for the first time. The devaluation was a major catalyst in the political watershed that ended the world's longest-lasting single-party state. The victory of *panista* Vicente Fox in the July 2000 presidential election was clearly the low point in the PRI's history. But it would be premature to write the party's obituary. The PRI still has advantages in experience and resources, and it is still the only party with a comprehensive organizational presence throughout Mexico. If the PRI does reinvent itself and return to power, however, it will do so within a democracy whose arrival was hastened by the PRI's own politically motivated policy errors.

Notes

1. The "Washington Consensus" represents general agreement among the U.S. government, international lending agencies, and mainstream economists that free markets and a reduced role for the state are the foundations of sustained growth in the developing world. See John Williamson, ed., *Latin American Adjustment: How Much Has Happened?* (Institute for International Economics, 1990).

2. *El inversionista mexicano,* August 29, 1994, p. 2. All dollar amounts are U.S. dollars.

3. *Wall Street Journal,* June 14, 1994, p. A6.

4. Douglas Payne, "Wall Street Blues," *New Republic,* March 13, 1995, p. 22.

5. Pedro Aspe, "Macroeconomic Stabilization and Structural Change in Mexico," *European Economic Review,* vol. 36 (1992), p. 325.

6. *El inversionista mexicano,* July 25, 1994; *El financiero,* November 3, 1994, p. 3A.

7. Celso Garrido, "National Private Groups in Mexico: 1987–1993," *Cepal Review,* vol. 53 (1994), pp. 159–75.

8. While foreign-owned *maquilas,* such as producers of autos and electronics, have traditionally imported the vast majority of their imports from the home country, domestic manufacturers are also major importers. From 1989 to 1993, while Mexican non-*maquila* exports rose 31.9 percent, from $22.8 billion to $30 billion, an annual increase of 7.2 percent, non-*maquila* imports rose by an astonishing 109 percent, from $23.4 billion to $48.9 billion, an average of 20.2 percent a year (*El inversionista mexicano,* August 29, 1994).

9. Timothy P. Kessler, *Global Capital and National Politics: Reforming Mexico's Financial System* (Westport, Conn.: Praeger, 1999), pp. 90–101.

10. Uhran Demirors, "Credibility of Exchange-Rate Policy Wins Foreign Investors' Favor in Latin America," *Latin American Money Markets* (supplement to *Latin Finance*) (January–February 1994) p. 6.

11. See Manuel Pastor, "Pesos, Policies, and Predictions," in Carol Wise, ed., *The Post-NAFTA Political Economy* (Pennsylvania State University Press, 1998).

12. Although similar to Mexican treasury bills, these bonds cannot be bought or sold on any market and cannot be used as collateral in financial transactions.

13. Less publicized provisions included increasing central bank autonomy, which was controversial because the sitting governor was former finance minister Guillermo Ortiz, widely accused of being responsible for the Fobaproa fiasco. Another provision, designed to lure foreign capital to the country's crippled banking system, was to remove remaining barriers to foreign ownership, which triggered some populist complaints about loss of national patrimony. Less controversial provisions included increasing the autonomy of financial regulators, scaling back the 100 percent deposit guarantee, and enforcing debt payment and collections.

14. *Wall Street Journal,* June 3, 1998, p. A11.

15. The basis for the accusation was article 9 of the Public Debt Law, which states that Congress will authorize the amount of net internal and external debt necessary to finance the government and other federal public entities. However, according to Attorney General Ismael Gómez Gordillo, because Fobaproa's assets were private, the bank rescue was not subject to the same rules governing public debt. See *Reforma,* June 2, 1998, p. 1; and *El universal,* August 7, 1998, p. 6.

16. *El financiero,* June 11, 1998.

17. *Los Angeles Times*, July 13, 1998, p. A11.

18. The vote was 325 to 159 in the lower house, with twelve *panistas* and seven *priístas* joining the opposition, and 93 to 10 in the PRI-dominated Senate.

19. *Boletín mexicano de la crisis*, December 19–25, 1998, p. 10.

20. Julia Preston, "Runaway Banks without Brakes," *New York Times*, July 22, 1999, p. 3.

21. See Geri Smith and Elizabeth Malkin, "Mexican Makeover," *Business Week,* December 21, 1998, pp. 50–52.

22. See Thomas W. Slover, "Tequila Sunrise: Has Mexico Emerged from the Darkness of Financial Crisis?" in *NAFTA: Law and Business Review of the Americas,* vol. 5 (Winter 1999), pp. 91–135.

23. One of the IPAB's first tasks was to create new rules that would enable banks holding nontradable government notes to swap them for tradable debt. Although the measure would increase the liquidity of the banking system and make more credit available to the private sector, it cannot improve the banks' capacity for risk analysis and it is unlikely to overcome their aversion to lending.

24. Quoted in Matthew Doman, "Crying Out for Corporate Funding," *Euromoney* (September 1998), p. 156.

25. Mark Stevenson, "Mexico to Subsidize Banks," *Associated Press*, June 9, 1999.

26. Henry Tricks, "Bank Seizure Is at Heart of a Tougher Mexican Strategy," *Financial Times*, June 23, 1999, p. 5.

27. James Smith, "Banking System Remains Mexico's Achilles' Heel," *Los Angeles Times*, June 24, 1999, p. C1.

28. Caroline Brothers, "Mexico's Serfin Cheaper to Save than Sink," *Reuters Financial Report,* June 28, 1999.

29. Argentina's proposal for dollarization was not taken very seriously by the international financial community or, more importantly, the United States, because Argentina's integration ties with the North American bloc are weak. Although a dollarized currency area for Mexico is certainly more plausible, given the rapid growth of economic ties between all three NAFTA countries, the response of the Zedillo administration suggests that it could take quite some time for domestic politics in Mexico to adapt to this idea. See J. P. Morgan, "Monetary Union in the Americas," *Economic Research Note,* February 12, 1999.

30. Adolfo Garza, "Mexican Businessmen, President at Odds over Dollarization," *Associated Press,* March 13, 1999.

4

ELIANA CARDOSO

Brazil's Currency Crisis: The Shift from an Exchange Rate Anchor to a Flexible Regime

THE COLLAPSE OF THE Brazilian real in January 1999 fits a familiar pattern of crisis in countries that target the exchange rate to stabilize inflation. In each instance, overvaluation leads to unsustainable current account deficits and eventual currency collapse. The pattern is hardly new—the Southern Cone countries had attempted similar stabilization schemes in the 1970s, and with the same results. Why, then, did Brazil pursue this strategy, particularly after Mexico exposed its limitations again in 1994? Was the case of Brazil different enough to warrant optimism about the outcome?

This is a story whose basic plot was foretold long before the real collapsed. A few investors misgauged the timing or extent of the devaluation, but not its inevitability. Most anticipated the outcome and profited handsomely. Policymakers themselves were neither naive nor cynical—a graceful exit strategy was simply not available. And, ironically, many would choose an exchange rate–based stabilization plan again if confronted with the same scenario.

This chapter looks for lessons from the Brazilian experience. The first section explores why an exchange rate anchor was adopted in 1994, and the second describes how this strategy led to its own demise. The third sec-

Thanks to Ann and Jean Helwege for their input and help in completing this chapter.

tion discusses the dynamics of central bank reserve losses, the decision to devalue, and the efforts to prevent the exchange rate from overshooting in its adjustment.

Why the Real Plan?

Sustained long-run growth—enough to warrant the use of the term "Brazilian miracle"—is a receding memory. Brazil's rapid growth after World War II ended in economic crisis and triple-digit inflation in 1964, but a period of sustained stabilization then followed. Despite the OPEC oil shocks of the early 1970s, high rates of economic growth prevailed, especially by regional standards. Between 1968 and 1980 the gross domestic product (GDP) per capita rose by over 6 percent a year. In the same period, exports became more diversified and grew by an average of 22 percent a year. High public savings and a fairly dynamic state enterprise sector also characterized the early half of this period. However, reliance on commercial loans to finance both public investment and expensive oil imports led to the debt crisis of the early 1980s. Since then, growth has faltered. Between 1980 and 1998, the annual real GDP growth rate was 2 percent, a mediocre performance for an economy that, since 1949, had grown on average 7.3 percent annually.

The end of rapid growth compounded distributional challenges posed by the transition to civilian rule in the 1980s. As the military ceded power and as literacy requirements for voting were lifted in the 1980s, Brazil's extreme income inequality quickly came to haunt democratic leaders.[1] State and federal budgets fell prey to the pent-up demands for greater equality unleashed by democratization. The Constitution of 1988 only exacerbated these fiscal pressures by incorporating numerous privileges for a host of special interests. With the capacity of future democratic regimes to mediate economic demands thus undermined, inflation became the main mechanism for managing imbalances that politicians could not or would not correct. Some of those imbalances are illustrated in figure 4-1.

Between 1981 and 1994 the annual rate of inflation exceeded 100 percent in all years except 1986. The reduction of chronic inflation therefore became the main focus of economic policy. Yet despite the failure of a spectacular series of stabilization plans that produced six monetary reforms in ten years, escalating inflation did not destroy the Brazilian economy. Instead, producers, consumers, and policymakers adapted to inflation

Figure 4-1. *Distribution of the Brazilian Government's Social Expenditures, 1999*

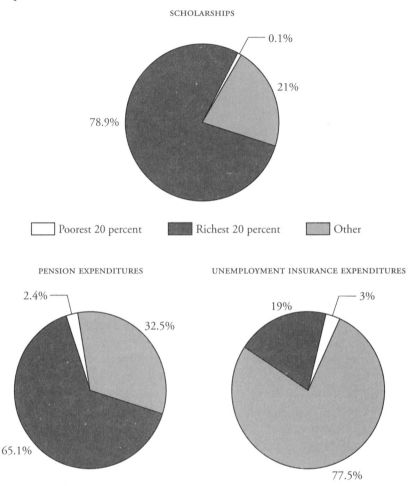

SCHOLARSHIPS

0.1%

21%

78.9%

☐ Poorest 20 percent   ■ Richest 20 percent   ▨ Other

PENSION EXPENDITURES

2.4%

32.5%

65.1%

UNEMPLOYMENT INSURANCE EXPENDITURES

19%

3%

77.5%

Source: Data from Instituto de Pesquisa Econômica Aplicada (IPEA), Brazil, 1999, cited in "Ipea: má qualidade de gastos sociais agrava problema da pobreza no país," *O Globo,* August 13, 1999.

through the pervasive use of indexation. Tax revenues did not fall significantly; indeed, they remained high relative to other Latin American countries. Moreover, Brazil's financial sector and industrial businesses functioned fairly well. Except during short periods, policymakers maintained exchange rate competitiveness and the country was able to generate substantial trade surpluses until mid-1994.[2] This capacity to accommodate inflation explains at least in part Brazil's failure to engage in serious structural change.

A ratchet pattern characterized the behavior of inflation in the late 1980s, when a series of heterodox policy interventions resulted in lower inflation rates for a few months, after which inflation climbed upward again. The Cruzado Plan began in February 1986 and lasted sixteen months. President José Sarney, who had succeeded President-elect Tancredo Neves on the latter's untimely death in April 1985, was in a weak position politically. His economic advisers convinced him that a heterodox shock program would stabilize the economy and win his administration popular support.

The plan froze prices, prohibited indexation in financial markets, and, after a wage increase, froze both wages and the nominal exchange rate. Lacking fiscal and monetary discipline and unable to arrest growing trade deficits, the government was forced to dismantle price controls and shift to a crawling peg exchange rate regime based on daily devaluations. Inflation returned and another stabilization attempt was imposed, the Bresser Plan of June 1987, which also relied on price freezes and a new wage indexation scheme. A standby agreement with the International Monetary Fund (IMF) was approved in 1988, but it failed because of Brazil's inadequate fiscal performance. In January 1989 the Summer Plan introduced yet another price and wage freeze, which was relaxed in April with a return to formal indexation. By early 1990, inflation was already running close to 3,000 percent a year.

In national elections at the end of 1989, a little-known political figure from the northeast, Fernando Collor de Mello, defeated the candidate of the Workers Party (PT), Luis Inacio da Silva ("Lula"), in a second round of voting. Collor had promised a new economic program, but details about its content were not forthcoming before his inauguration in March 1990. In the face of inflation that could no longer be accommodated through indexation, the Collor Plan of March 1990 sought to reduce prices through drastic cuts in liquidity. An arbitrary freeze was imposed for seventeen months on nearly two-thirds of the money supply, broadly defined to include demand deposits, mutual funds, federal bonds, state and municipal bonds, saving deposits, and private bonds. Although Brazilians eventually managed to circumvent some of these controls, a financial freeze that took over personal assets was understandably unpopular. The plan also contained important components of structural reform, including trade liberalization and privatization of nonperforming public enterprises, which were sustained throughout the decade. By 1992, however, President Fernando Collor was ousted from power in a corruption scandal, and inflation continued its upward spiral.

By the time Collor left office in December 1992, the economy's resilience had been sapped.[3] Another standby agreement with the IMF in January 1992 temporarily shifted economic policy in a more orthodox direction, with an emphasis on fiscal and monetary tightening. This change was short-lived, however; nominal interest rates fell in 1993, budget deficits expanded, and inflation accelerated. The IMF standby agreement expired in August 1993 and was not renewed. As inflation exceeded 2,000 percent, the Real Plan was launched in December 1993.[4] The vice president, Itamar Franco, a populist at heart, had succeeded Collor de Mello. Four finance ministers held brief succeeding tenures but proved unsatisfactory; finally Fernando Henrique Cardoso was appointed to the post. Cardoso quickly assembled a young talented team of economists and planned a new approach to controlling inflation. The plan changed the name of the currency to the *real*, hence the name of the new policy.

Under the Real Plan, stabilization went through three stages: a brief fiscal adjustment, monetary reform, and the use of the exchange rate as a nominal anchor. In January 1994 Brazil's Congress approved a fiscal adjustment plan that included cuts in current spending and the creation of an Emergency Social Fund. The fund was financed by redirected federal revenues—that is, new limits on the ability of states and municipalities to access credit and the recovery of mandatory social security contributions—that allowed the government to sever some of its mandated links between revenues and expenditures. Twenty percent of revenues that had been earmarked for other purposes was freed. This increased flexibility led to an operational surplus in 1994.

The second component of the Real Plan, a temporary monetary reform measure, linked contracts, prices, wages, and the exchange rate to a single daily escalator and unit of account, the *unidade real de valor* (URV), while the *cruzeiro real* remained in circulation. The adjustment, which started on March 1, 1994, lasted four months. Because the *cruzeiro real* and the URV depreciated relative to the U.S. dollar at roughly the same rate, most prices and contracts were set implicitly in U.S. dollars. Finally, on July 1, 1994, a new currency, the real, was introduced by converting contracts denominated in URVs into reals at a rate of one to one. The *cruzeiro real* ceased to exist, and was converted at CR$2,750 per R$1. Cardoso used the success of the Real Plan to campaign successfully for the presidency at the end of 1994.

Policy Quagmires under the Real Plan

The Real Plan brought inflation under control with remarkable speed: it fell from four digits in 1994 to two digits in 1995 and to less than 2 percent in 1998. Indeed, Fernando Henrique Cardoso's success in securing the right to run for reelection in 1998 drew on the widespread popularity he derived from sustained price stability. Economic growth was also strong: GDP growth averaged 4 percent a year between 1994 and 1997, compared to flat or declining output in the previous five years. The economic boom that began in 1994 did not originate in a decline in real interest rates, as happened in the first phases of other exchange rate–based disinflation programs. In fact, real interest rates remained high throughout the period. Between June 1995 and December 1998, the passive real interest rate averaged 22 percent a year.

Instead, the Brazilian boom appears to have originated with an increase in real wages. Between 1993 and 1995 several wage adjustments (including increases in minimum wages and in government wages and salaries) took place. These gains in income were reflected in booming imports and durable goods consumption.[5] High real interest rates drew in capital to finance growing imbalances. Nevertheless, because the anchored exchange rate appreciated under high interest rates and heavy capital inflows, Brazilian policymakers faced complex and often contradictory policy choices as they attempted to sustain growth against the backdrop of rising fiscal and trade deficits and volatile capital flows.

Fiscal Deficits: Primary, Operational, Quasi, and Invisible

The Real Plan started with a stated commitment to control fiscal deficits, but any fiscal adjustment achieved in 1994 quickly lost steam. The operational deficit, which includes real interest payments on debt, moved from a surplus in 1994 to a deficit equal to 5 percent of GDP in 1995; it remained around 4 percent of GDP in 1996 and 1997 and deteriorated further in 1998. The primary surplus, which excludes interest payments, declined in 1995, reflecting a significant increase in payroll outlays, and turned into a deficit in 1996. Factors that contributed to the primary imbalance included a 43 percent increase in pensions following the increase in the minimum wage in May 1995 and the significant growth of "other expenditures," particularly as the 1998 elections approached.[6] In 1998 the budget deficit reached 8 percent of GDP.

Fiscal problems were compounded by the emergence of substantial quasi-fiscal deficits in federal and state banks. For example, the federally owned Banco do Brasil (the agricultural sector's traditional source of subsidized credit) and the National Bank of Development introduced programs of subsidized credit to exporters in 1996. Partly to finance these programs, the treasury recapitalized Banco do Brasil by R$7.9 billion (over 1 percent of GDP). Such intergovernmental transfers contributed to an increase of total net public debt from 30 percent of GDP in 1995 to 35 percent in 1996.[7]

Furthermore, with the end of inflation, bad loans that state banks had made to state governments became a serious problem. For example, the federal government agreed to swap its own bonds for the obligations—about R$33 billion—of São Paulo to BANESPA, one of the state banks of São Paulo. Although this action did not directly increase the net federal debt because federal bonds were offset by state obligations, such measures to stabilize weak state banks further increased the federal government's vulnerability to capital shocks. Although the economy was growing on average by more than 3 percent a year between 1994 and 1998, the ratio of net public debt to GDP increased from 28 percent in 1995 to 44 percent in 1998; it jumped to more than 50 percent after the devaluation in January 1999. It should be noted that the state banks have been central to the politics of patronage and clientelism for decades in Brazil. They often served as a means to finance political campaigns at the state and local level. It was a delicate challenge for the new government to both seek the support of state governors for its stabilization program and simultaneously undercut a traditional source of political influence.

The end of inflation also made fiscal problems more transparent. High real interest rates did undermine fiscal efforts, but it was the numerous spending loopholes embedded in the Constitution of 1988, the failure to rein in excessive pension payments, and increased expenditures during the 1998 election year that lay at the core of fiscal fragility in the second half of the 1990s.[8] Before the launching of the Real Plan, unresolved distributional issues had been masked in policy deliberations by passing infeasible budgets, with inflation serving as the equilibratory mechanism. With the end of inflation, policymakers had no choice but to undertake structural reforms to contain fiscal deficits. However, much remains to be done. Reform initiatives must overcome resistance to structural change. A pertinent example is Brazil's social security system, which is an important contributor to the government's fiscal deficit, and which can only be described as extraordinary. Its main characteristics are as follows:[9]

—Many Brazilians have longer retirements than careers

—The average Brazilian retires at forty-nine

—In the public sector, about two-thirds of retiring civil servants in 1998 were younger than fifty-five, and 14 percent were younger than forty-five

—In the private sector, nearly 4 percent of the more than 400,000 workers retiring in 1997 were in their thirties

—In 1999, benefits paid to public and private sector retirees ran nearly $30 billion in the red, equivalent to 5 percent of economic output and more than twice the government's spending on health care

—Seventy-five percent of the 1999 budget deficit came from benefit payments to just 3 million of Brazil's 20 million retirees: government bureaucrats

—The social security deficit is the largest contributor to the budget gap and continues to grow, despite recent minor reforms

Repeated efforts to curb the drain on the federal budget by reducing retirement benefits have met with little success. Politicians are loath to reduce entitlements that constituents believe have been mandated for them and for their families.

The Temptation to Use Monetary Policy as a Substitute for Fiscal Reform

Tight monetary policy, including higher reserve requirements and stringent lending restrictions, was supposed to support stabilization. The increase in required reserves, coupled with the lowering of inflation, did lead to a substantial decline in deposit banks' inflationary reserves. Also, the tighter lending restrictions resulted in an increase in the central bank's share of total seigniorage from an average of 60 percent in the first half of 1994 to 84 percent a year later. (The share in GDP of seigniorage seized by deposit banks consequently fell from 2 percent to nearly zero.)[10]

The increase in required reserves and the decline in the banking sector's seigniorage explains, in part, rising interest rate spreads and high active real interest rates. Required reserves were gradually reduced, but other factors—taxes on financial transactions and the increase in nonperforming loans caused by higher real interest rates after stabilization, for example—helped keep the spreads high.

Because stabilization was not achieved through a tightening of fiscal policy, which would have in turn reduced financing of the deficit through seigniorage collected by the central bank, the burden of adjustment fell disproportionately on monetary policy. Seigniorage collected by the central bank rose from 1.8 percent of GDP in 1993, the peak inflation year, to 3 percent in 1994, the year of the Real Plan; it stood at 2 percent in 1995—the level of average seigniorage during the years of high inflation.[11]

This appropriation of seigniorage from the banking sector to the central bank helped finance government spending as inflation ebbed, but it also put the banking sector at risk. A more balanced policy would not have transferred the revenues from money creation so drastically from deposit banks to the central bank, and thus would have avoided the increase in interest rate spreads and nonperforming loans. As it was, however, banks' weaknesses were exposed, particularly those of public banks, and the need for restructuring placed further strains on fiscal resources. Since July 1994 the central bank has intervened in 51 banks and 140 other financial institutions.

Trade Policy: Balancing Liberalization and Stability

During the early 1990s, Brazil followed the lead of other Latin American countries and opened trade by reducing tariffs, eliminating nontariff barriers, and abolishing subsidies on exports. These unilateral measures were bolstered by Brazil's participation in the Southern Cone Common Market, or Mercosur. In January 1995 Mercosur's common external tariff became effective. Common external tariffs, which now range from zero to 20 percent and are applied on about 85 percent of Mercosur's trade with the rest of the world, impose discipline by making it more difficult to reverse liberalization measures. But the direct impact of Mercosur on the Brazilian economy will be small: only 16 percent of Brazil's exports trade within the bloc, and the country's total trade (imports plus exports) amounts to only 7 percent of GDP. Nonetheless, engagement in the Mercosur process signaled Brazil's broader commitment to market reform and to an export-led development strategy based on greater trade competitiveness.

Mercosur also played a role in the democratic transition in the mid-1980s, allowing two new and weak chief executives—Raúl Alfonsín in Argentina and José Sarney in Brazil—to reduce military tensions and budgets. It also ended the historical enmity between the two countries, which had been rooted in old geopolitical goals no longer relevant at the end of the century.

Partly as a result of unilateral trade liberalization, the average tariff rate fell from more than 30 percent in 1991 to 14 percent by the end of 1994. Both nominal and effective protection declined and became more uniform between 1991 and 1994. The combination of unilateral liberalization and exchange rate appreciation became perilous. The trade balance, which for ten years had been in surplus, showed a deficit during the last two months of 1994 that persisted throughout 1995 and contributed to a rising current account deficit. Because Brazilian-Argentine trade ties had strengthened under Mercosur, the appreciation of the real against the peso further fueled these deficits. To the chagrin of its Mercosur partners, Brazil increased tariffs on imports of motor vehicles in 1995. In 1996, a new round of tariff cuts was made on a number of goods, while tariffs were increased on textiles and toys.

When Mexico's crisis hit in December 1994, Brazil's high foreign reserves gave the economic authorities some latitude in choosing how to respond. Still, the Mexican shock hit Brazil at a delicate moment, forcing Brazilian policymakers to attend to the country's rising trade deficit. And it came just as the Cardoso administration was taking office in Brasília. The trade deficit further increased through 1995 as the Real Plan spurred the expansion of domestic demand. Financial instability in early 1995 forced policymakers to reorder priorities. Devaluation—which would have forced the necessary adjustment in relative prices—was ruled out as a risky invitation to full-blown contagion of the peso crisis. Instead, the economic authorities adopted fiscal and monetary measures in March 1995 to control aggregate demand and to improve the balance of payments. Fiscal measures included spending cuts for federal and state enterprises, restrictions on federal payroll outlays, and changes in legislation to increase tax revenues (for example, income taxes were levied on dividends from financial investments).

The government took measures to control credit growth, including a mandatory 60 percent deposit with the central bank on bank assets used for collateral guarantees and select loans, an increase in the tax rate from 6 percent to 18 percent on financial operations involving bank loans (including negative balances on credit card debts and promissory notes), a prohibition on financial intermediation involving commercial paper by banks, and an increase in the reserve requirement for time deposits.

On the external side, the Ministry of Finance abolished the taxes imposed in October 1994 on the purchase of Brazilian equities by foreigners and on foreign credit transactions. The tax on foreign investments in Brazilian fixed-income funds was reduced to 5 percent. The central bank adopted a new exchange rate band and devalued the currency by 5.2 percent against the dollar. Because this devaluation was too small to significantly affect the trade balance, however, other tools—perceived as less likely to ignite inflation—were employed. Industrial exporters received additional incentives through tax reductions on domestic inputs, and tariffs on certain durable consumer goods and vehicles were temporarily increased from 20 percent to 70 percent.

The policy measures had the desired outcome. Economic growth slowed, and by August 1995 the monthly trade balance was positive, contributing to a reduction of the accumulated trade deficit in twelve months. The trade balance improvement was a result of the recession, however, and would be lost in the recovery that followed in the second half of 1996—itself underpinned by the continued appreciation of the Brazilian real against the Argentine peso.

Exchange Rate Management: The Missing Exit Strategy

Brazil's success in bringing down inflation was associated with real exchange rate appreciation. Between 1994 and 1998, the average real exchange rate was 31 percent above the average of the previous fourteen years; the only comparable peaks occurred before the debt crisis of 1982 and in the wake of failed heterodox plans.

Despite minor devaluations between 1995 and 1998, the real exchange rate at the end of 1998 was still as high as it was at the beginning of 1996. There were no structural changes or anticipated growth to justify such a significant real appreciation. On the contrary, sustained long-run growth would have been inconsistent with the large current account deficits that were bound to prevail at the going real exchange rate. The behavior of the trade balance reinforces this observation. During 1995 Brazil's trade deficit increased during the first semester and started to decline during the second semester as the economy contracted. But a small recovery after June 1996 was enough to produce further deterioration. The trade balance continued to worsen, producing a deficit of $8.4 billion in 1997 and $6.5 billion in 1998. Evidence of overvaluation was also apparent in the slow growth of exports. Between 1995 and 1998, the growth rate of exports in dollar terms was 4.2 percent a year compared to an average of 11.3 percent a year between 1991 and 1994.

The strong currency harmed the industrial sector and increased unemployment. The government reacted by channeling subsidized credit to exporters through the National Development Bank and by approving legislation to exempt primary and semimanufactured exports from indirect taxes (manufactured goods were already exempt from indirect taxes). Neither measure was sufficient to offset the effects of overvaluation.

This phenomenon of accumulated real appreciation has been evident in other Latin American stabilization programs using the exchange rate as a nominal anchor: in Chile during the period 1975–81, in Mexico during 1987–93, and in Argentina during 1990–95. Among the early experimenters with neoconservatism, Chile fixed its exchange rate to reduce inflation. The result was a real appreciation, sizable capital inflows, large external deficits, and, in 1982, a sharp devaluation and recession. Mexico and Argentina more recently followed a similar stabilization path, reducing inflation by using an exchange rate anchor, building up fiscal surpluses, pursuing trade liberalization, and supporting privatization. Both countries enhanced productivity by reforming goods and labor markets, but growth in productivity is rarely enough to counterbalance an overvalued exchange rate.

The problem with exchange rate overvaluation is that it is often associated with a boom in consumption involving a large increase in imports and a decline in private savings. An overvalued exchange rate encourages agents to bring forward imports that they fear may become more expensive later. When this takes place at the same time as trade liberalization, its effects are multiplied, leading to a jump in imports as controls are dismantled. If reforms face a credibility problem, firms and households doubt that trade liberalization will be maintained and go on a precautionary import binge. For these reasons, a boom in imports is often characteristic of periods of economic reform. Even where exports have grown fast, as they did in Mexico during the early 1990s, exchange rate anchors tend to foster trade deficits.

A second, less obvious problem with overvaluation is that it encourages a decline in private savings as residents substitute present for future consumption. Mexico's exports were growing strongly in 1994, but national savings had declined to very low levels (13.7 percent of GDP).[12] Between 1978 and 1981, a low level of savings, averaging just 10 percent of GDP, also characterized overvaluation in Chile.[13] By undermining savings, overvaluation hinders economic activity because high interest rates are needed to maintain the capital inflows to support the exchange rate. As growth dwindles, savings decline further, leading to a vicious circle of low savings and low growth.

Both of these problems—growing trade deficits and declining savings—emerged in Brazil. Imports nearly doubled between 1994 and 1997, driven partly by the appreciation of the real against the Argentine peso. Combined with the slower growth of exports, the trade balance turned from a healthy surplus of $10 billion to a deficit of $8.4 billion.[14] At the same time, gross national savings declined from 19.7 percent of the GNP in 1994 to 16.8 percent in 1997.

The Mexican experience, confirmed by Brazil in 1999, showed that the costs of real appreciation compound slowly but explode suddenly.[15] The run on the Mexican peso highlighted the risks that arise when foreign capital sustains exchange rate overvaluation and current account deficits. In Brazil, as in Mexico, the crisis took years to develop because interest rate policies allowed overvaluation to persist. As long as reserves and capital flows are available, the temptation to continue to use the exchange rate to keep inflation under control seems irresistible.

Capital Flows: Maintaining Credibility as the Fundamentals Deteriorate

Although they eventually reduced domestic savings and created unsustainable current account deficits, monetary and exchange rate policies under the Real Plan led to a boom in capital flows that initially helped stabilization. Capital flows averaging $39 million a month between 1988 and 1991 mushroomed into a monthly net flow of $970 million between 1992 and 1995. In 1996 and 1997, total net annual capital flows reached $33 billion and $26 billion, respectively. Accumulating reserves, fed by capital flows, masked the severity of the current account deficit and the decline in private savings. As capital continued to enter Brazil, it sustained currency overvaluation and clouded policymakers' perception of the maturing crisis. In the end, by supporting exchange rate overvaluation, these capital flows helped bring about the collapse of the economy.

In the two years before the inception of the Real Plan, Brazil's interest rate differentials vis-à-vis the United States far exceeded expected currency depreciation in the short run and attracted foreign capital. A desire to counteract the pressure of exchange rate appreciation in the face of large, potentially volatile capital inflows led to central bank intervention. Capital controls were used to discriminate between investment believed to make the economy more productive and competitive (such as foreign direct investment) and potentially volatile investment motivated by considerations of short-term gains. Authorities turned restrictions on and off during the 1990s, applying selective taxes to limit such capital inflows.[16]

The Brazilian evidence is consistent with that of other countries, indicating that controls can generate interest rate differentials for extended periods of time.[17] Capital controls have also changed the composition of flows in Brazil, at least temporarily. They have been less effective in monitoring the quantity of flows or in avoiding the final collapse of the real. To avoid a monetary expansion induced by capital flows, inflows were partly sterilized. Sterilization created significant fiscal costs in financing high levels of reserve holdings, both because of the scale of the operations and the size of the interest differential vis-à-vis U.S. dollar rates (and rates in other reserve centers). The rise in monetary authorities' gross foreign assets in relation to the increase in the monetary base suggests that sterilization operations were large and costly in Brazil in the 1990s.

The unsustainability of such a situation should not have been in doubt, yet few governments can resist the temptation to let the real exchange rate appreciate as long as money is flowing in to finance current account deficits. The common argument is that productivity growth in the tradable goods sector is enough to justify real appreciation, and that the current account deficit reflects capital good imports that will generate future exports to pay for the accumulated liabilities. The hard truth is that productivity growth in the tradable goods sector would have to be well above what is credible to justify the real appreciation that occurs at the beginning of exchange rate–based stabilization programs. Domestic politics, moreover, would have to be much more conducive to the kinds of competition policies that would help to accelerate productivity gains in Brazil. Under a freely floating exchange rate regime, the risk of such optimism is borne by private portfolios. Under an exchange rate–based stabilization scheme, the government's self-deception entails an increasingly expensive commitment to guarantee an untenable outcome.

When the Mexican peso crisis erupted in late 1994, the initial reaction of investors suggested that Mexico's financial crisis would compromise all emerging markets as stock prices plunged, particularly in Argentina and Brazil. During the fourth quarter of 1994 and the first quarter of 1995, the net flow of capital into Brazil was insufficient to finance the current account deficit, and the central bank lost reserves of about $9.8 billion.

The rescue operation led by the United States and the IMF to support Mexican reform successfully insulated financial markets from the crisis and capital returned to Brazil. By the end of 1995, net capital flows were up to $29 billion, and in 1996 they reached $33 billion.

Although the Real Plan survived the Mexican shock, by mid-1995 policymakers faced the same fundamental challenges as before that event. In broad terms, insufficient fiscal adjustment continued to impose a burden on monetary, credit, and exchange rate policies. In particular, interest differentials increased sharply and remained high. These unusually high real interest rates partly reflect the difficulty of establishing the credibility of macroeconomic policy in a country that has a history of hyperinflation and where fiscal balance has been held hostage to congressional politics.

High interest rates accompanied a sharp increase in the debt of the public sector. In 1995 the stock of central bank securities and treasury securities outside the central bank grew by 53 percent in real terms.[18] Between 1994 and 1996, the ratio of the net debt of the public sector to GDP increased from 28.5 percent to 35 percent, as high real interest rates allowed a weakening of the fiscal stance for two consecutive years. Net debt continued to grow in the following years, reaching 44 percent of GDP in 1998.

Lack of confidence in the ability of the regime to sustain the exchange rate anchor and to meet its obligations was reflected in the increasing use of dollar-denominated and floating-rate debt. Before the problems of 1998, most domestically denominated debt was at fixed rates, and about 15 percent was indexed to the dollar. By early 1999, 21 percent was dollar-denominated and 70 percent was indexed to the overnight interest rate. The interest due on domestic debt in January 1999 alone exceeded 6 percent of GDP.

Controlled Spin: Managing the Collapse of 1999

As noted earlier, the Mexican crisis led to a significant loss of investor confidence, but this was restored as Mexican policymakers moved assertively to stabilize the economy. The 1997 Asian crisis caused a brief panic, but the real jolt came with the Russian devaluation and debt default of August 1998. Brazil's foreign currency reserves fell by $30 billion as the government struggled to defend the real in the face of another major external shock.

The IMF moved quickly to set up a loan package, but domestic politics, including the timing of presidential and gubernatorial elections and the tense relationship between the central and state governments, delayed these negotiations. Finally, in December 1998 Brazil signed a $41.5 billion financial assistance package. Contributions were to come from the IMF ($18 billion), the World Bank and the Inter-American Development Bank ($4.5 billion each), and bilateral creditors ($5 billion of which would be provided by the United States and $9.5 billion by European governments). In light of the crisis intervention role that the IMF had played in other currency disruptions and the very mixed results that had been achieved, its approach with Brazil was of a more preventive nature. About $9.2 billion was disbursed in mid-December 1998 from this multilateral package. Further disbursements were conditional on compliance with a three-year IMF standby program, which focused on fiscal adjustment. The initial program aimed at reducing the public sector borrowing requirement from 8 percent of GDP in 1998 to 4.7 percent in 1999.

The IMF program gave the Brazilian financial sector time to reduce its external exposure. It was soon overtaken by events, however, as monetary policy failed to prevent a collapse of the exchange rate. Capital outflows, lack of fiscal progress, strong resistance by the domestic business community to record-high interest rates, and growing demands for correction of the overvalued exchange rate forced the government to adopt a new exchange rate regime. The real was set free to float on January 15, and by the end of February it had depreciated by more than 35 percent. In the three-week period between January 13 and February 2, through a combination of the weaker real and high real interest rates, twenty-four banks saw a $10 billion profit from sale-and-buy operations in the futures exchange. Citibank and Morgan Guaranty Trust had the largest stakes in operations in the futures exchange. The big loser was Banco do Brasil, operating on behalf of the central bank.[19]

Interest Rate Policy: Preventing the Real's Free Fall

Although most economists would agree that the real has been overvalued since the launching of the Real Plan, there is no consensus on the size of the overvaluation. After the collapse, the average real exchange rate in the first quarter of 1999 was close to that which prevailed before the implementation of the Real Plan. But it was not stable: between mid-January and the end of March, the real's value against the dollar fluctuated to as high as 2.2 before settling at 1.68 in early May.

The new exchange rate regime allowed the government to adopt a more balanced policy mix, but it imposed the need for a new monetary framework and a new nominal anchor. The most difficult problem was in setting monetary policy during the first few weeks after the collapse of the exchange rate, when financial market conditions and expectations were unsettled.

Inflation can increase sharply after a speculative attack on the currency, because substantial depreciation causes a one-time adjustment in many prices. This temporary increase in inflation would then reduce real interest rates on debt denominated in domestic currency, and thus fuel capital flight. To offset, at least partially, this near-term effect, it is appropriate for policymakers to raise nominal interest rates to avoid further depreciation and the danger of igniting a spiral of depreciation and inflation. On the other hand, policymakers also have to pay attention to the debt denominated in foreign currency. The larger that debt, the greater the impact of the devaluation on the debt-to-GDP ratio. In the case of Brazil, that ratio had reached 53 percent by January 1999.

The Brazil-IMF agreement announced on March 8, 1999 set two clear objectives: to limit the inflationary impact of the devaluation by raising interest rates and to prevent the ratio of debt to GDP from exploding by producing substantial primary surpluses in the fiscal accounts. The agreement recognized that the likely cost of these policies would be a recession and estimated a decline in GDP of 3.5–4 percent. Discussion centered around a strategy that critics called contradictory: the reliance on high interest rates to control inflation, which at the same time aggravated the fiscal deficit by increasing the debt burden and reducing tax revenues. And, of course, higher real interest rates can lead investors to fear that the government will not be able to service its debt and will thus resort to the printing press or, equally bad, that the government will not be willing to risk the political fallout of a severe recession.

However, once an exchange rate anchor is abandoned, inflationary expectations will again set in. After a collapse of the currency, the central bank must tighten monetary policy to avoid the deadly spiral of devaluation, inflation, and further devaluation. If monetary policy is too loose, people will use cash to buy dollars, bringing about more devaluation and more inflation. Interest rates would have to increase.

In the aftermath of the January 1999 devaluation, Brazilian policymakers were faced with the question of how high interest rates should be raised.

If the central bank raises interest rates too little too late, inflation picks up and the economy returns to its history of persistent inflation. Inflation might once again hide some structural imbalances, but it would certainly destroy external confidence. If the central bank increases the interest rate too much, the resulting recession might be too severe and inflation could decline ahead of interest rates, leading to higher real interest rates. The combination of recession and high real interest rates would increase the budget deficit and reduce confidence in the government's capacity to service its debt without again resorting to monetization. Moreover, the prospect of a severe recession can undermine confidence in the government's resolve to sustain tight monetary policy, and thus set off a new round of inflationary expectations.

Since fundamentals are never as dark or as bright as painted, the recovery of credibility is everything. As the government raises interest rates, inflationary expectations must be declining for markets to bring nominal interest rates back down. But if there is a large public debt that is both short term and carries floating interest rates, as in Brazil, investors may worry that higher interest rates will force the regime into debt monetization.

The short-run task, then, is to negotiate a path of declining inflation and interest rates to avert a collapse of the exchange rate that overshoots its new equilibrium level. Failure to stay within this path has implications for the budget, and vice versa: the smaller the primary deficit, the greater the latitude policymakers will have in setting monetary policy. However, it is difficult to achieve dramatic changes in the primary budget, especially when politics are entrenched, constitutional amendments are required, and operational deficits—which reflect interest payments on outstanding debt—may thus be outside the regime's control. For this reason, support from multilateral institutions can be essential for restoring credibility and stability.

Brazil: Dancing Away from the Precipice

By any standard, Brazil has navigated its way through the real crisis with extraordinary ease and speed. By May 1999 the real had risen to 1.67 to $1, compared to a low of 2.21 in March.[20] Short-term interest rates had fallen from 45 percent in March to 23 percent by May, and inflation, measured by the national consumer index, had declined from an annualized rate of 16 percent in March to 6 percent in April. Far from slipping into a deep recession, the Brazilian economy actually grew by 1 percent in the first quarter of 1999, and forecasts of a serious decline in output were being revised.

What explains the rapid turnaround? Certainly a dose of good luck has to be acknowledged. Interest rates in the United States remained low, and agricultural output grew by 18 percent in the first quarter of 1999, thanks to a record harvest following good weather conditions. But central to the restoration of investor confidence was fiscal action and shrewd monetary policy. Awareness of the risk of a grave collapse among even intransigent legislators and governors helped: by February, the collapse of the real had galvanized Congress into passing pension reform legislation that it had rejected in 1998. Congress also approved an increase in a temporary tax on financial transactions and introduced measures to rein in expenditures by state and local authorities.[21] By the end of the first quarter of 1999, the central government had a primary fiscal surplus of $5.6 billion.

Monetary policy played the critical role. Following the inflationary shock of the mid-January devaluation, prices immediately increased, pushing real interest rates down. The central bank reacted by raising interest rates, which turned into extraordinarily high real interest rates in March. As inflationary expectations fell, nominal interest rates were allowed to decline. Yet real interest rates in April and May were still among the highest in the world. This strategy successfully shifted the economy from a potentially explosive situation to a path of steadily declining inflation, allowing real interest rates to decline gradually.

The central bank demonstrated its commitment to restraining inflation through tight monetary policy, even as official forecasts pointed to a 4 percent contraction in GDP and unemployment was rising.[22] This resolve partially restored confidence, and by April short-term capital was flooding back in, attracted by the high yields in Brazil's financial markets.

External endorsement of these measures by multilateral institutions lent credibility. In March the government of Brazil and the IMF announced that they had agreed on a revised economic program. The IMF strongly supported the government's commitment to keeping inflationary expectations low, protecting expenditures on social programs, and maintaining the programs of structural fiscal reform on which credibility and the recovery of growth would be based. Once the fiscal measures that had been rejected in the fall were ratified, the central bank could confidently count on access to the remainder of its $41.5 billion in IMF credit. The World Bank's contribution of $4.5 billion went to support social spending and state-level reforms.

Brazil's banking sector was also a factor in this recovery: many banks had anticipated the devaluation and had both positioned themselves to profit from it through currency-futures contracts and hedged by holding dollar-linked government bonds. As a result, the risk of a banking sector collapse did not threaten fiscal balance, as it had in Asia and Mexico. The agility of the financial sector in assessing and acting on changes in inflation also facilitated the steady reduction in interest rates. Renewed capital inflows allowed the central bank to reduce nominal interest rates six times in seven weeks without creating the impression that it was abandoning tight monetary policies.

The Transition from Crisis Management to Sustained Growth

By the end of May 1999, Brazilian markets were once again shaken by contagion, this time from the country's immediate neighbor to the south. Despite efforts by Argentina's government to slay rumors that it would be forced to abandon its currency board, which since 1991 has fixed the exchange rate one-for-one against the U.S. dollar, markets remained jittery. Brazil's success in stopping a spiral of rising inflation and depreciation of the exchange rate will entail more than the recovery of a profitable stock market. Provided there is no outbreak of major financial market turbulence or excessive delays on the fiscal front, the economy will continue to expand through 2000. Averting recession will undoubtedly be the main concern of Brazil's 70 million people who live in poverty; will they be at least no worse off as a result of the central bank's gamble pitting their livelihood against the fickle opinion of world financial markets?

Brazil still faces the challenge of defining a credible economic strategy for the future. By delicately managing the relationship among interest rates, inflation, and exchange rates, policymakers have temporarily contained speculative attacks on the real. However, a return to sustained high growth is less certain. Complicating the question of sustained growth is the lack of progress in resolving the distributional issues that underpin Brazil's fiscal deficits. The illusion that macroeconomic growth under the Real Plan can satisfy all competing demands is gone. At the same time, the international investment community is increasingly agile in the face of currency risk and potential default. Brazil's next steps must look less like a quick fix and more like steady progress toward resolution of its fundamental problems.

Yet substantial reforms have eluded Brazil for more than a decade. The operational deficit is still large because of accumulated interest obligations, and external finance remains vital to service external liabilities accumulated during the past five years. Should exports fail to pick up briskly within the next year, confidence could wane.

Even more potentially damaging are the corruption scandals that threaten the credibility of the government at all levels. They also undermine confidence in the ability of Congress to move beyond solutions to the budget deficit that rely on distortionary measures such as the financial transaction tax. The overall tax burden is not small by Latin American standards, but revenues are not progressively collected and spent. One unfortunate result of regressive tax policy and inadequate investment in human capital is that the average level of education in Brazil—which is as low as that of much poorer countries—restrains productivity growth.

The realization of sustained rapid growth will require more targeted investment in human capital, deep institutional reform of the state, and the restraint of special interests that undermine economic progress. When will Brazil return to the challenge of these more enduring reforms? Without the successful containment of the real crisis, one could not have even posed this question, but it is not likely that new crises can be averted unless fundamental reforms are brought forward and carried out.

Conclusion

This chapter has offered three main insights into exchange rate policy in Brazil. The first is the essential role of fiscal reform in the use of the exchange rate as a nominal anchor. During the lengthy pre-stabilization era in Brazil, inflation helped render the budget deficit manageable, even though in hindsight it was not. The second is, in the absence of deep fiscal reform after the Real Plan was launched, policymakers were left to rely on public borrowing and high real interest rates to support the exchange rate. Even though Brazil maintained an active monetary policy and one of the developing world's highest levels of reserves during 1994–98, the growing fiscal and current account deficits still worked to unhinge the exchange rate anchor. The final point, which is similar to Mexico's experience, is that financial markets in Brazil recovered much more quickly than expected. While the recovery has been a welcome relief, it is important not to be overly optimistic. Much of the returning capital is still short-term and, in contrast to Mexico, Brazil's external opportunities for export growth are still rather restrictive. Most important, although the recovery from the January 1999 devaluation was quicker than expected, several formidable tasks still lie ahead. These include deep structural reform and fiscal stream-lining, as well as the crafting of a viable pro-reform political coalition to counter the numerous conflicting interests that worked to cause the financial crash of January 1999.

Notes

1. Brazil's Gini coefficient (a measure of income inequality in a population in which the larger the coefficient, the greater the inequality) is among the highest in the world.

2. The exceptions occurred in 1986, when the exchange rate was fixed, and in 1989 and early 1990, when inflation accelerated and the mini-devaluations lagged behind as an overt policy effort to slow down inflation.

3. GDP declined by 4 percent in 1990 and again by 0.5 percent in 1992.

4. At the same time, the fall of international interest rates eased the external debt burden and led to an April 1994 agreement with creditor banks that covered over $50 billion in debt stocks and arrears.

5. See José De Gregorio, Pablo Guidotti, and Carlos Vegh, *Inflation Stabilization and the Consumption of Durable Goods* (Washington: International Monetary Fund, 1994).

6. "Other expenditures" is an item in the central government budget that includes investment and miscellaneous current expenditures (*outras despesas de custeio e capital,* known as OCC) to which the treasury allocates resources in proportion to congressional appropriations. It is this "other expenditures" category that creates an arena for fiscal bargaining between the national administration and politicians.

7. The recognition of liabilities, such as R$25 billion for the Fundo de Compensação Variação Salarial (a mortgage guarantee fund) and R$21 billion for the Fundo de Garantia de Tempo de Serviço (an unemployment and disability fund for workers), as well as write-offs of bad assets in public banks, will further increase total net debt in the medium term.

8. On the effect of high real interest rates, see Eliana Cardoso, "Virtual Deficits and the Patinkin Effect," *IMF Staff Papers,* vol. 45 (December 1998), pp. 619–46.

9. *Wall Street Journal,* September 9, 1999, p. A1.

10. See Cardoso, "Virtual Deficits."

11. A decline in total seigniorage collection was matched by a decline in seigniorage collection by the commercial banks, while seigniorage collected by the central bank was unchanged. Thus there was no wealth effect from the decline in inflation but only a transfer between the banking sector and the nonbanking sector. In 1996, though, the central bank's seigniorage did decline to 1 percent of GDP.

12. For an overview of the Mexican crisis, see Moisés Naím, "Mexico's Larger Story," *Foreign Policy,* vol. 99 (Summer 1995), pp. 112–30.

13. Gian Maria Milesi-Ferretti and Assaf Razin, "Current Account Sustainability," *International Journal of Finance and Economics,* vol. 1 (July 1996), pp. 161–81.

14. All dollar amounts are U.S. dollars unless otherwise noted.

15. See Ilan Goldfajn and Rodrigo Valdés, "The Aftermath of Appreciations," Working Paper 5650 (Cambridge, Mass.: National Bureau of Economic Research, July 1996).

16. See Eliana Cardoso and Ilan Goldfajn, "Capital Flows to Brazil: The Endogeneity of Capital Controls," *IMF Staff Papers,* vol. 45 (March 1998), pp. 161–202.

17. See Maurice Obstfeld, "International Capital Mobility in the 1990s," in Peter Kenen, ed., *Understanding Interdependence: The Macroeconomics of the Open Economy* (Princeton University Press, 1995), pp. 201–61.

18. Associação Nacional das Instituições do Mercado Aberto, *Retrospectiva 1995* (Rio de Janeiro), table 3.6.

19. So said Deputy Aloizio Mercadante in testimony to the parliamentary committee investigating irregularities in Brazil's financial system.

20. But on May 24, 1999, it was down again to 1.72, indicating that stability is still in the making.

21. To deal with state government debt, the federal government entered into new types of restructuring agreements. These agreements impose conditionality on state governments, requiring an increase in primary surpluses by reducing payrolls and privatizing local concerns. New legislation foresees liquidation and privatization of state banks, but also allows for their recapitalization. It also imposes a ceiling on debts of state governments, forbidding state banks to buy new securities issued by local governments. The debt rescheduling agreements with the states target a decline in the ratio of the stock of net domestic debt to state revenue (net of transfers to municipalities) from an average of 200 percent to 100 percent by 2006.

22. The official unemployment rate has risen sharply from an average of 5 percent during 1990–97 to an average of 8 percent from 1998 through June 2000 (Instituto Brasiliero de Geografia e Estadistica). This figure excludes many people who would regard themselves as out of work, such as those who were not actively looking for a job during the specific week in the month when the survey was taken. A survey by DIEESE (a union-backed research group) uses a broader measure and puts the unemployment rate at 20 percent of the work force in greater São Paulo.

5

CAROL WISE

Argentina's Currency Board:
The Ties That Bind?

S INCE THE MID-1980s all of the larger emerging market countries in
Latin America, with the exception of Argentina, have shifted from fixed
exchange rates, which peg the domestic currency to one or more foreign
currencies, to more flexible regimes under which the value of the currency
is determined more or less by supply and demand for it in the market.
Apart from Argentina, it is the smaller states in the Caribbean (such as
Barbados, Dominica, and Grenada) and Central America (Panama, for
example) that continue to adhere to fixed exchange rate arrangements.[1]
This trend in the western hemisphere reflects the developing world in general: by 1996 countries with fixed rates accounted for just 2 percent of the
developing world's total trade, compared with 70 percent in 1975.

Although the question of which exchange rate regime is more appropriate is still actively debated by academics and policymakers, these trends
speak for themselves to a certain extent. Why, then, has Argentina, with its

Background research for this chapter was supported by the North-South Center at the
University of Miami, the U.S. Institute of Peace, and the Fulbright Commission in Buenos
Aires. The author thanks John Hipp for his excellent data gathering and analysis, as well as
Isaac Cohen, Max Corden, Carol Graham, Randy Henning, Tim Kessler, Maureen Molot,
Ron Scheman, Judith Teichman, and two anonymous reviewers for their helpful comments
on earlier drafts.

large emerging market, remained steadfastly committed since 1991 to a fixed rate regime now more commonly associated with small, open economies that lack the capacity to run a monetary policy independent of their trading partners? Given the pivotal role that flexible exchange rates were assigned within the market reform package advocated by the "Washington Consensus," Argentina's holdout status is doubly puzzling, because this is a country that has otherwise sought to follow Washington's prescriptions to the letter.[2]

The debates over fixed versus flexible exchange rates are ambiguous: one side offers strong justification for Argentina's adoption of a fixed exchange rate, while the other is equally convincing about the need to shift to a more flexible regime.[3] At stake is the question of how a country can best promote growth, productivity, and income gains; withstand external shocks and maintain a balance in international payments; and minimize adjustment costs in terms of output, employment, and inflation. As Max Corden notes in his chapter, arguments in favor of a fixed currency arise when a country has lost all credibility in signaling a strict commitment to low inflation and macroeconomic discipline. When the disturbances impinging on an economy are predominantly monetary, an "anchored" exchange rate that fixes the currency to that of another country with a history of low inflation may be the only way to establish the necessary credibility.

This was precisely the situation in which Argentina found itself when the government launched the Convertibility Plan in April 1991. When monthly rates of inflation suddenly burst from the 20 to 30 percent range in the late 1980s to 90 to 200 percent in 1989–90, the administration of President Carlos Menem had little choice but to pursue one of the most credibility-enhancing strategies available to a country in the throes of hyperinflation: a currency board.[4] Under the currency board, the Argentine peso was fixed one-to-one to the U.S. dollar, and full convertibility was established between the two currencies. At the same time, the discretionary lending powers of the Argentine central bank were sharply curtailed, and the bank was required to maintain foreign reserves totaling 100 percent of the domestic monetary base. The Convertibility Plan effectively tied the hands of domestic policymakers, as the currency board shifted the burden of responsibility for monetary policy and, to a lesser extent, fiscal restraint onto the external sector.

This minimal room to maneuver has fueled other arguments about the need for greater exchange rate flexibility. The trend toward greater flexibility has been associated with more open, outward-oriented trade and investment policies across the developing world, as well as with high levels of international capital mobility in the 1990s. The success of the Argentine strategy in reducing inflation and restoring macroeconomic stability in the face of increased international volatility is indisputable. However, it is difficult to ignore the trade-offs: the peso's steady real appreciation, the loss of trade competitiveness, and rising current account deficits, all of which have contributed to unprecedented double-digit levels of unemployment. In light of these trade-offs, advocates of more flexible arrangements insist that it is less costly to pursue balance-of-payments adjustments through reliance on a flexible exchange rate mechanism. Under a more flexible regime, the costs of an unsustainable policy can become more readily apparent through movements in real exchange rates and prices. Consequently, a flexible regime can exert equally strong discipline on policy.[5]

Debates over fixed versus flexible exchange rates have been further clouded by the fact that neither ranks above the other in terms of macroeconomic performance in the 1990s. During the period following the 1982 debt crisis, inflation appeared consistently lower and less volatile in countries with fixed rates, but this gap has narrowed over the past decade.[6] Thus the notable shift toward greater flexibility appears to result from the fact that considerations affecting the choice of an exchange rate regime tend to change over time. As the chapters in this volume by Timothy Kessler and Eliana Cardoso show, when Mexico and Brazil were each suffering from high inflation, policymakers aptly perceived that fixed rates were the key to a successful stabilization effort. Yet when this task was accomplished, other challenges arose. External disequilibria mounted under the pressures of currency appreciation and surging capital inflows, leaving both countries little choice but to opt for floating rates that allowed for more flexibility in adjusting to external imbalances.

Interestingly, since Mexico's 1994 peso crisis, Argentina has stood several times on the same precipice of currency appreciation and external volatility that prompted Mexico to abandon a fixed exchange rate. And now, in the wake of Brazil's January 1999 devaluation, Argentina finds itself out on another economic ledge. Nevertheless, although the conditions that initially prompted the adoption of a rigidly fixed exchange rate have changed markedly, Argentine policymakers have again declared their intention to stay the course with the currency board rather than shift to a more flexible and potentially less costly strategy. The remainder of this chapter explores why. After briefly reviewing the reform track record under the

Convertibility Plan, as well as policymakers' ability to defend the peso in the face of continual external volatility that began with the tequila shock of 1995, the chapter then turns to longer-term considerations regarding the development of the Argentine political economy in the convertibility era.

The Heyday of the Convertibility Plan, 1991–94

While shocking to most Argentines, the country's bout with hyperinflation during 1989–91 represented the culmination of nearly forty years of state-led economic mismanagement and political turmoil.[7] In contrast to the prolonged periods of high growth and exchange rate stability witnessed during Brazil's "miracle" years that began in the 1960s, or Mexico's buoyant postwar expansion under a model of "stabilizing development," Argentina remained the odd one out. Despite its status as the third largest economy in the region, from 1950 to 1991 low growth, high inflation, and chronic fiscal deficits consistently plagued the country.[8] Elected on the Peronist ticket in 1989, the Menem administration struggled unsuccessfully for nearly two years to reverse these long-standing trends. As annual inflation approached 5,000 percent in 1989 and public finances collapsed, Argentines, in national opinion polls, cried out for relief. It finally became clear that the resolution of a crisis of this magnitude would require an equally dramatic response.

As a first step, Menem distanced himself from the staunch interventionist influences that still prevailed within his own Peronist party, or Partido Justicialista (PJ), and openly declared his allegiance to an ambitious program of market reform. Similar to other political leaders in the region who had been noncommittal about their reform preferences before their election, and then more pragmatic once the realities of macroeconomic stabilization had set in, Menem surprised his own supporters within the ranks of organized labor and domestically oriented business by forging ahead with a formidable program of liberalization, privatization, and deregulation. Like these other leaders—for example, Venezuela's Carlos Andres Perez and Peru's Alberto Fujimori—Menem was immediately pressed to broaden his coalitional bases in ways that would induce more powerful, internationally oriented private sector actors to join the reform program. Hence Menem's early reliance on a team of technical advisers associated with the country's largest transnational firm, the Bunge and Born Group, and, subsequently, the appointment of Domingo Cavallo as finance minister in early 1991. As an economist who commanded respect in both domestic and international financial circles, Cavallo not only masterminded the Convertibility Plan but also became its single most important guarantor in the eyes of foreign investors.

The Convertibility Plan of 1991, which fixed the Argentine peso to the U.S. dollar under a currency board, emerged as both the centerpiece of the Menem team's stabilization effort and as one of several policy components in a broader package of market-based structural reforms. Two earlier key pieces of legislation enacted by the Menem administration had already signaled the seriousness of Argentina's commitment to economic restructuring along market lines: the Economic Emergency Law and the State Reform Law, both passed in 1989, went to the heart of the fiscal morass in which Argentina had been mired since the end of the first administration of Juan Peron in the mid-1950s. The former bill suspended the complex scheme of manufacturing subsidies and preferences that had been the cornerstone of Argentine protectionism and authorized dismissals for redundant public sector personnel; the latter laid the legal groundwork for the full-scale privatization of the country's debt-ridden state enterprises, including companies in the telephone, airline, railroad, shipping, highway, and petrochemical sectors.[9]

Thanks to the strength of the Peronist bloc in the Argentine Congress, the executive branch had been delegated the power to legislate further tax, trade, and regulatory reforms by executive decree.[10] The tax system was redesigned around a value added tax and an expanded income tax, widespread exemptions were eliminated, and institutional mechanisms for compliance and collection were strengthened. On the trade front, Argentina pursued a two-pronged strategy: the unilateral liberalization of tariffs, with strong backing from multilateral institutions in the late 1980s; and the pursuit of further trade barrier reductions through participation in the Southern Cone Common Market (Mercosur), launched by Argentina, Brazil, Paraguay, and Uruguay in the early 1990s. By March 1991 the average tariff had been reduced to 10 percent (11 percent on industrial inputs and 22 percent on manufactured goods). Later that year, these tax and trade measures were followed by sweeping regulatory reforms. The petroleum market and foreign investment regimes were completely liberalized, and restrictions were pared down on numerous internal markets (communications, transportation, agriculture, and the Buenos Aires stock exchange).

Simultaneously, the Cavallo team worked to shore up the financial base necessary to render the Convertibility Plan viable. The team had anchored the nominal exchange rate to the U.S. dollar and prohibited any currency emissions not backed by hard reserves in the central bank; the task ahead was to accumulate a level of international reserves conducive to a non-inflationary increase in liquidity and economic activity. Although the country's international reserves were limited at the outset of the plan, the widespread dollarization of the Argentine economy under hyperinflation made it easier for the government to back up the domestic monetary base with foreign exchange.[11] The lowering of U.S. interest rates in 1991 facil-itated the further accumulation of foreign exchange, which prompted investors to seek higher returns in emerging markets such as Argentina's. This development, combined with the aggressive divestiture of state assets and the long-awaited repatriation of flight capital from abroad, expanded Argentina's foreign reserve base from $2.4 billion in March 1991 to more than $6 billion by year's end.[12]

Given the seemingly endless string of failed stabilization plans that the country had endured up to this point, even the architects of the currency board were caught off guard by its short-term success. From 1991 to 1994, the Argentine economy enjoyed its longest and most robust expansion in the entire postwar period. Average annual inflation rates were reduced from 84 percent in 1991 to 3.9 percent in 1994; during this same time frame, GDP grew at an average annual rate of 7.7 percent, consumption at a yearly rate of 8.6 percent, and real investment at a yearly rate of 22 per-cent.[13] Under the impetus of increased revenues generated through Cavallo's radical reform of the tax system, and with an extra boost from this consumption-led boom, the primary (noninterest) balance of the federal government shifted from a deficit of 10.5 percent of GDP in 1989 to a sur-plus in 1992 and 1993.[14] By 1994, this combination of price stability, cap-ital inflows, and expanding foreign exchange reserves had enabled the eco-nomic team to slash interest rates by half. In turn, easier access to capital financed a significant expansion of Argentine growth and investment, as shown in table 5-1.

It was the context of severe economic crisis that had allowed President Menem to move more boldly than any of his contemporary predecessors on the reform front, and it was the overwhelming success of this first phase of stabilization that enabled the government to cement a powerful reform coalition, one that looked nothing like the union-based, nationalist-populist supporters who had been so instrumental in electing Menem on the Peronist ticket in 1989. It would later become evident that it was through the delay in implementing market reforms at the provincial level of government and the maintenance of "illiberal enclaves" such as the heavily regulated labor market that the fundamental reforms (liberalization, privatization, convertibility) were made politically viable.[15] Nevertheless, by simultaneously reaching out to big business interests, the middle classes, liberal-minded technocrats, and consumers at large, Menem broadened his bases of support in ways that did appear to have clipped the more traditional wings of Peronism once and for all. With the Convertibility Plan becoming the focal point for a more centrist pro-stabilization political alliance in Argentina, Menem moved with ease toward his 1995 bid for reelection. However, Mexico's unexpected financial debacle in late 1994 quickly shifted the center of political and economic gravity in Argentina: the currency board, and the efforts of Menem and his economic advisers to salvage it, were soon put to an extreme test.

Defending the Currency Board, 1995–99

Even before the contagion from the Mexican peso crisis, or the "tequila shock," struck Argentina, the Convertibility Plan and the broader reform program that framed it had begun to show some strains. Despite the impressive pace of economic stabilization, inflation in Argentina was still higher than it was in the United States during the 1991–94 period. The result, as depicted in table 5-1, was a steady real appreciation of the peso, which was immediately reflected in the 1992 trade deficit figures. The fiscal scenario was also troublesome, as public revenues derived disproportionately from the more regressive value added tax. Tax revenues had improved markedly because of the boom in consumption, but public expenditures also remained high. Low savings rates (public and private) during this period suggested that neither the government nor the Argentine consumers had abandoned their pro-cyclical tendencies to overspend when economic times were good. Perhaps the biggest surprise was the unemployment rate, which rose from 7 percent in 1990 to 12 percent in 1994. Certainly some job losses had been predicted in the context of the privatization drive, but it had also been expected—at least by outside observers—that these losses would be offset by the liberalization of Argentina's heavily regulated labor markets. The fact that the decade-long Menem administration never pursued this objective with much conviction reflects the ways in which the executive was still beholden to his earlier roots in the Peronist party.

Table 5-1. *Macroeconomic Indicators in Argentina, 1981–99*

Indicator	1981	1983	1985	1987	1989	1991	1993	1995	1997	1998	1999
Real GDP growth	-5.4	4.1	-6.9	2.6	-6.9	12.7	5.9	-2.8	8.1	3.9	-3.3
Real per capita GNP growth	-8.3	2.3	-9.5	1.0	-12.3	11.3	4.5	-4.2	6.7	2.6	n.a.
Inflation[a]	104.5	343.8	672.2	131.3	3,079.8	84.0	7.4	1.6	0.3	0.7	-1.4
Total domestic investment[b]	22.7	20.9	17.6	19.6	15.5	14.6	18.3	17.9	19.4	19.9	n.a.
Private investment[b]	16.9	14.8	12.5	15.7	12.2	12.7	16.6	16.4	17.9	18.2	n.a.
Public investment[b]	5.8	6.1	5.1	3.9	3.3	1.9	1.7	1.5	1.4	1.7	n.a.
Real exchange rate[c]	75.1	157.0	163.0	95.8	191.2	72.5	55.6	54.2	55.0	53.2	54.3
Trade balance[d]	712	3,716	4,878	1,017	5,709	4,419	(2,364)	2,357	(2,123)	(3,117)	(829)
Current account[e]	(4,712)	(2,436)	(952)	(4,235)	(1,305)	(647)	(8,030)	(4,985)	(11,954)	(14,274)	(12,152)
Foreign direct investment[e]	730	187	919	(19)	1,028	2,439	2,059	3,818	5,099	4,344	20,000
Foreign portfolio investment[e]	1,125	649	(617)	(572)	(1,098)	(34)	33,731	1,864	11,087	8,339	(6,618)
Total external debt[e]	35,657	45,920	50,946	58,458	65,257	66,028	65,325	99,363	130,828	144,050	145,050

Sources: Data for GDP, GNP, and debt are from the World Bank's *World Tables* (CD-ROM, 1999, 2000); except 1998 GDP and GNP per capita, from the Inter-American Development Bank website (www.iadb.org), and 1998 debt from the joint website of the Bank for International Settlements, the International Monetary Fund (IMF), and the Organization for Economic Cooperation and Development (www.oecd.org/dac/debt). Data on investment are from Jack D. Glen and Mariusz A. Sumlinski, "Trends in Private Investment in Developing Countries: Statistics for 1970–96," data set available on the World Bank's International Finance Corporation website. Data on inflation, exchange rates, and payments are calculated from the IMF's *International Financial Statistics* (CD-ROM, June 1999); except trade balance and current account data for Argentina prior to 1976, from the IMF's *1984 International Financial Statistics Yearbook*, and FDI and portfolio investment data for Argentina prior to 1976, from the *1994 International Financial Statistics Yearbook*.

n.a. Not available.

a. December to December.

b. Percentage of GDP.

c. 1990 = 100, calculated using period average exchange rate, U.S. wholesale price index, and domestic consumer price index.

d. Merchandise exports minus merchandise imports, in millions of U.S. dollars.

e. Millions of U.S. dollars.

The 1995 Tequila Shock

By early 1995 the downside of the Convertibility Plan was apparent. Whereas fortuitous external factors from 1991 to 1994—including low interest rates and high levels of international liquidity—had helped fuel Argentina's recovery, the reversal of these trends in late 1994 abruptly halted the economic expansion. Investors' fears over Mexico's possible default on its massive short-term debt had provoked not only a run on the Mexican peso but also a swift flight of capital from Mexico and other emerging markets in similar straits—that is, markets demonstrating real exchange rate overvaluation, burgeoning current account deficits, and growing debt obligations. The rapidity and force with which these foreign shocks were transmitted to the Argentine economy should perhaps have been expected, given the Convertibility Plan's intentional reliance on "automatic" external adjustments. Nevertheless, in early 1995, as bank deposits dropped by 17 percent and $5.5 billion flowed out of the country, policymakers found themselves scrambling to defend the currency board. Total losses for 1995 amounted to 4.6 percent of GDP, including a 6.4 percent contraction in industrial production. And, as table 5-1 shows, the total external debt had increased by one-third between 1991 and 1995, a sign of the extent to which the Convertibility Plan's high return on growth depended on external borrowing.

The adjustment options available under the currency board were limited, but in the end effective in reassuring investors of Argentina's commitment to a liberal economic model based on a fixed exchange rate. In the short run, interest rates were quickly hiked to halt the capital outflow, and the government was forced to cut more than $1 billion from the national budget in 1995 alone. Once the intensity of the crisis began to abate, the Menem team had to confront three major reform issues that restrictions inherent in the Convertibility Plan made all the more urgent. First, having stripped the central bank of its role as lender of last resort, the authorities could no longer overlook the weaknesses and disarray still present in the domestic banking system. Thus 1995 marked the beginning of a deep restructuring of the banking sector, such that a year later deposits exceeded their levels in the financial system before the tequila shock. In contrast to Mexico, where a full-blown banking crisis has exacerbated subsequent adjustment efforts since 1994, Argentina's determination to move aggressively on this front provided a crucial cushion against future financial shocks.

On the fiscal front, increased tax collections, expenditure cutting, and a revamping of the social security system were clearly necessary first steps in rationalizing fiscal policy, but these alone were not sufficient. In the wake of the tequila shock, it had become obvious that virtually no progress had been made in reforming fiscal policy at the provincial level. Moreover, the lingering contrast between fiscal resolve at the federal level and outright laxity within the provincial governments had periodically derailed Argentina in its attempts to meet the fiscal targets agreed upon with the International Monetary Fund (IMF). Indeed, provincial public expenditures before the 1995 shakeout had actually increased by more than 13 percent a year—a further sign that Menem hadn't entirely abandoned the old-style patrimonial tactics of Peronism. This delay in the streamlining of provincial budgets, and in the privatization of numerous state-held regional entities explains Menem's continued popularity in the regions once his welcome had clearly worn thin among voters in Buenos Aires. It also sheds light on the apparently sudden wrath that provincial constituents turned on the federal government once the fiscal adjustment finally hit the regions in 1995.

The remaining challenge lay in the adjustment of relative prices when the currency board ruled out real exchange rate devaluation as a viable option. Faced initially with the declining competitiveness of the exchange rate and pressure from exporters to reverse this trend, the government sought to address the growing trade deficit through a combination of higher tariffs and export subsidies. At the same time, the economic team sought to offset the peso's real appreciation by encouraging rapid gains in productivity. Although labor productivity figures did expand by an average of 4.1 percent from 1991 to 1995, so too did the unemployment rate. With the latter peaking at 20 percent in 1995, productivity gains obviously still depended too heavily on personnel layoffs and company downsizing, while efficiency continued to lag. As luck would have it, under the thrust of rising commodity prices and new demand for Argentine goods in Brazil when that country's Real Plan kicked in, the 1995 trade balance shifted into surplus. No matter that the relative price problem remained—the economic team considered itself vindicated by the quick turnaround in growth and investment shown in table 5-1 and by the $8.4 billion loan package granted to Argentina by the multilateral institutions in 1995.

By mid-1996 Menem's confidence in the Convertibility Plan was such that he finally fired Cavallo, putting an end to five years of daily public antics and acrimonious rivalry between the two men. After some initial fluctuation, markets held in the face of this news, as Menem replaced Cavallo with Roque Fernández, a former central bank staff member and supporter of convertibility and liberal economic reform. At this point the Convertibility Plan crossed an important threshold: its credibility no longer depended on the reputation and prestige of just one official, but rather on the country's reform track record. With the 1997 growth rate hitting 8.4 percent, it appeared that the tequila shock had been a temporary disruption from which the restructured Argentine economy had emerged all the stronger. As it turns out, however, although Argentina had clearly escaped from the unfortunate "ax-relax-collapse" syndrome that Javier Corrales attributes to the Venezuelan case (see chapter 6), the country had gotten back on its feet just in time for another round of external shocks.

Asian Spillovers, Russia's Default, and Brazil's Devaluation

In rapid succession, the authorities were confronted with a series of destabilizing currency devaluations that began in mid-1997 across Asia; by further financial contagion from Russia's devaluation and debt default in 1998; and by the 40 percent devaluation of the Brazilian currency in early 1999. Although the impact of the Asian contagion and the Russian meltdown definitely took a toll on Argentina, the figures in table 5-2 show that the force of these shocks did not approximate the damage suffered from the Mexican devaluation. The main side effects of these subsequent shocks were rising real interest rates and a plunge in asset prices, but this time around domestic and foreign capital did not flee the country. The resistance of the Argentine economy to another full-blown financial crisis can be attributed to the progress of fiscal and banking sector reform in the aftermath of the tequila shock, the latter spurred by the heightened participation of foreign banks in the country's financial system.

By 1998 Argentina's fiscal deficit was low by Latin American standards (1.3 percent of GDP), and short-term public debt seemed manageable at 3 percent of total public sector liabilities. The country's total external debt was running at a hefty 50 percent of GDP, although good overall performance still made it fairly easy for Argentina to borrow abroad. Moreover, and in stark contrast to Mexico, Argentina had developed a framework for bank supervision and consolidated its banking system to the extent that the financial sector ranked among the most sophisticated in the region.[16] Although aggregate growth dropped to around 4.2 percent of GDP in 1998 and unemployment continued in the 13 to 14 percent range, the

Table 5-2. *Impact of Shocks on Argentina's Economy during the Convertibility Era*

Indicator	Mexican devaluation	Cavallo resignation	Asia spillover	Russian default
Monetary variables				
Portfolio shift (percentage points)[a]	7.1	2.7	2.9	3.3
Reserve loss (percent)	−35.6	−9.8	−4.9	−5.4
Total deposits (percent)	−20.4	−1.6	3.3	1.8
Financial assets				
Equity (percent)	−45.7	−18.2	−33.2	−37.6
External debt	1,623	156	405	884
Currency risk[b]	1,244	207	308	279

Source: "Data Watch Argentina," *Global Data Watch* (Morgan Guaranty Trust), January 15, 1999, p. 21.
a. Increase in dollarization: dollar certificates of deposit as a percentage of total certificates of deposit.
b. Peso-dollar spread, thirty-day certificates of deposit.

country's ability to weather these shocks further bolstered the currency board's credibility. If anything, with Argentina becoming the first emerging-market country to return to international capital markets after the Asian and Russian disruptions, the currency board became a permanent fixture in the minds of voters, politicians, and policymakers. If not a perfect arrangement, convertibility had certainly become the preferred one.

It was not until the Brazilian devaluation of January 1999 that rumors of a possible shift to greater flexibility in the exchange rate began to surface in Buenos Aires. These claims, combined with increased speculation over interest rate jumps in the United States, sent Latin American stock markets into a tailspin. The Menem administration quickly denied the rumors, declaring that it would move to full dollarization of the economy if markets lost confidence in the peso, rather than abandon the currency board. The response from U.S. policymakers on the dollarization proposal was polite but not especially encouraging. (Because of the lack of strong trade and investment ties between Argentina and the United States, the more likely candidates for a dollarized currency area would be the United States, Canada, and Mexico, and even that is considered a possibility of the far distant future.)[17]

The perceived need for renewed credibility of the currency board in the wake of the Brazilian shock stemmed, first, from the widening peso-dollar

Table 5-3. *Forecasts for Argentina after Brazil's Devaluation*
Percent, except as indicated

Indicator	1998	1999
Real GDP	4.3	−3.2
Real consumption and inventories	4.1	−1.6
Fixed investments	7.2	−8.0
Real export of goods and services	7.0	−5.0
Real import of goods and services	8.5	−7.0
Consumer prices	0.9	−1.0
Current account balance (U.S.$ billions)	−12.5	−12.1
Percent of GDP	−3.7	−3.7
Merchandise trade balance (U.S.$ billions)	−6.0	−5.3
Government balance (U.S.$ billions)	−3.9	−5.4

Source: "Data Watch Argentina," *Global Data Watch* (Morgan Guaranty Trust), January 29, 1999, p. 19.

spreads on prime lending rates in 1999; and, second, from the highly adverse impact that the Brazilian devaluation was projected to have on the real economy (see table 5-3). In contrast to the Mexican, Asian, and Russian crises, which had all been transmitted to the Argentine economy through the financial system, the main transmission vehicle for the Brazilian shock was the real economy. Whereas the expansion of Argentine exports into the Brazilian market (attributable to the appreciation of the Brazilian real against the peso) had been important for the Argentine economy—and hence the recovery from the 1995 crisis—the bilateral trade balance now swung in the opposite direction.

By late 1998 Brazil accounted for 23 percent of Argentine imports and 30.5 percent of its exports. As the devaluation of the real pushed the bilateral exchange rate of the peso up by nearly 18 percent in real terms, the burden of adjustment quickly fell on Argentina's tradable sector. This unfavorable shift in relative prices was exacerbated throughout 1999 by the appreciation of the U.S. dollar, to which the currency board is anchored. With industrial production shrinking by 9.5 percent through the first three quarters of 1999, and disequilibrium in the trade and current account figures growing, it became evident that the usual fiscal and monetary tightening that had served the Convertibility Plan so well in the past would not by itself suffice to reverse these negative trends. Some respite was gained by the IMF's agreement to loosen up on Argentina's 1999–2000 fiscal targets, as deep recession again drove tax collections below projected levels. Earlier fiscal projections also were rendered unrealistic by the impending (October 1999) presidential elections, never a propitious time to restrain government spending, and certainly not in the context of yet another economic crisis.

The Brazilian devaluation engendered the same dilemma that had been swept under the carpet by the Menem team in the midst of the 1996 economic turnaround: how can relative prices be adjusted under a fixed exchange rate regime that prohibits devaluation? The obvious answer is to pursue a real exchange rate adjustment through rapid productivity gains that can boost the country's competitiveness. Yet the Argentine Congress had failed to deliver even the most basic requirements for achieving these goals, such as lower labor and tax costs for businesses. Predictably, this absence of concrete productivity-enhancing incentives from the government, coupled with the flood of Brazilian goods into the domestic market, gave rise to new demands for protectionism on the part of the Argentine private sector.[18] At the same time, without abandoning their allegiance to the Convertibility Plan, private sector groups became more vocal in their calls for competitive policies to better complement the currency board. At the top of their list were demands for the lowering of interest rates for working capital, a reduction in the 35 percent tax on profits, cheaper rates on freight and services, and more flexible labor regulations to reduce the hefty "Argentine cost" of doing business.[19]

The Transformation of the Argentine Economy under a Fixed Exchange Rate

The differences between the political economy in the pre-reform period and that in Argentina today are so vast that a prospective investor returning after a decade's absence would be hard pressed to believe them. In this respect, the results of Argentina's sweeping program of market reforms have been remarkable. Across sectors, barriers to competition have been reduced and the Argentine economy is now a considerably more stable, transparent, and predictable place to do business. However, nearly a decade into the market reform effort, the longer-term outcomes are still mixed. The main difficulties that Argentina now confronts are (1) persistently high unemployment rates and a worsening of income distribution; (2) pending problems surrounding competition, regulation, and the oversight of domestic markets; and (3) the lack of a clearly defined development strategy reflecting more than the shorter-term stabilization and adjustment imperatives that have dominated policymaking since the launch of the Convertibility Plan. In the midst of the 1999 recession, for example, the absence of a concrete strategy for economic reactivation exacerbated problems—such as a record-setting debt-service ratio of 60 percent—that once seemed under control.

Turning to the first point, table 5-4 captures the extent to which the Menem administration's ability to stabilize prices and trigger a steady pattern of growth and investment has failed to filter down to the everyday lives of working people. Argentina's comparatively high levels of unemployment in the 1990s reflect the cumulative impact of privatization, antiquated labor market rules, and the deleterious effect of relative price distortions. Because state firms have traditionally accounted for just 3 to 4 percent of the country's total employment, privatization is perhaps of less concern than other causes of unemployment. A more compelling explanation for the problem is high nonwage labor costs and numerous restrictions on hiring and dismissal, which prevailed during Menem's decade-long tenure in office. In theory, the introduction of greater labor market flexibility should accelerate sectoral adjustments, allow for a more efficient allocation of resources, relieve the pressure on the exchange rate, and trigger greater employment expansion.[20] But this, unfortunately, has not been the chosen path. Instead, the peso's appreciation since 1991 has channeled economic resources toward more capital-intensive activities in the nontradable sector, where efficiency gains have been uneven and labor markets remain distorted and depressed.

As table 5-4 shows, the trend toward worsening income distribution in Argentina corresponds with a regionwide pattern in the 1990s. However, the greater income losses suffered by the poorest 40 percent of the Argentine population have been exacerbated by the unfavorable scenario just described. In regional terms, the deterioration in income shares is related, first, to a widening gap in education and skill differentials and, second, to increased levels of asset concentration since the onset of liberalization.[21] On the first count, although Argentina's population still ranks among the most highly educated in the region, one significant legacy of the 1980s is the deterioration of the quality of and access to training and educational opportunities. This decline has been compounded by the increased presence of foreign firms in the Argentine economy in the 1990s, primarily in the services sector, and the propensity of these investors to transfer up-to-date technology and production practices that reach beyond

Table 5-4. *Growth, Investment, and Distributional Returns in Argentina, Brazil, Chile, and Mexico, Selected Years, 1986–99*

Indicator	Period	Argentina	Brazil	Chile	Mexico
GDP growth	1990–99	4.2	2.5	5.8	3.4
Gross domestic investment/GDP	1990–98	17.7	20.8	25.3	22.9
Exports/GDP[a]	1990–98	8.9	8.6	29.9	23.0
Percent change in consumer prices over previous year	Dec. 1999	–1.8	8.4	2.3	12.3
Real wages[b]	1990–99	0.0	0.5	3.7	0.8
Employment[b]	1990–98	1.3	1.5	2.2	3.0
Labor productivity[b]	1990–95	4.1	–0.1	3.3	–2.2
Urban unemployment[c]	1990–98	11.6	5.4	7.3	3.8
Education gap[d]	1994	1.9 (1996)	4.7	1.5	3.1
Percent of national income accruing to					
Poorest 40 percent	1986	16.2	9.7	12.6	12.7 (1984)
	1990	14.9	9.6	13.4	11.7 (1989)
	1994	13.9	11.8	13.3	10.8
	1996	14.9	10.5	13.4	10.8
Richest 10 percent	1986	34.5	44.3	39.6	34.3 (1984)
	1990	34.8	41.7	39.2	39.0 (1989)
	1994	34.2	42.5	40.3	41.2
	1996	35.8	44.3	39.4	42.8

Sources: GDP data are from the website of the Economic Commission for Latin America and the Caribbean (ECLAC) (www.ECLAC.org). Gross domestic investment data are from World Bank, *World Development Indicators* (CD-ROM, 1998). Export data are calculated from respective national accounts data from IMF, *International Financial Statistics* (CD-ROM, September 1998). Consumer price data are from "Emerging Markets: Economic Indicators," Morgan Guaranty Trust Company, New York, various issues. Data on real wages are from ECLAC, *Preliminary Overview of the Economy of Latin America and the Caribbean, 1997.* Employment, labor productivity, and urban unemployment data are from "Latin American Growth, Poverty, and Inequality," *CEPAL News,* vol. 7 (1997), no. 27, pp. 1–3, and ECLAC's website. Education data were presented by Jere Behrman, Nancy Birdsall, and Miguel Székely at the Workshop on Social Mobility, Brookings Institution, Washington, D.C., June 4–5, 1998. For the distribution of national income, Chilean and Brazilian data based on urban areas and Argentine data based on Buenos Aires are from ECLAC, *The Equity Gap* (1997); Mexican data on monetary income are from Manuel Pastor and Carol Wise, "Mexican-Style Neoliberalism," in Carol Wise, ed., *The Post-NAFTA Political Economy* (Pennsylvania State University Press, 1998).

a. Exports include goods and services.
b. Average annual growth rate.
c. Average annual rate.
d. Average number of years behind in school, ages fifteen through eighteen.

the skills of the average Argentine worker. Thus the odds of sinking for the first time into the poorest 40 percent of the working population are significantly higher.

The increased concentration of productive assets in post-privatization Argentina has further contributed to this growing structural heterogeneity. In principle, state firms were divested under the guidelines of formal antitrust legislation; however, hindsight shows that the political will of the Menem administration to combat monopolistic business practices has been nil. As the dust settled on the mass of privatizations that were completed from 1991 to 1994, sixty-six of those companies that had been privatized suddenly appeared on Argentina's list of the top two hundred companies.[22] Moreover, fifty companies in this newly privatized group quickly came to account for 60 percent of the total profits generated by the top two hundred firms. In 1995 just three of these privatized firms accounted for 40 percent of the total turnover of the seventy companies listed on the Buenos Aires stock exchange.[23] Asset concentration of this magnitude does not bode well for those smaller- and medium-size firms in the productive sector that lack the capital and know-how to compete effectively. It bodes even worse for the Argentine worker, because it is these smaller companies that have traditionally provided the main impetus for job creation.

Apart from its adverse distributional consequences, this disturbing pattern of business concentration also highlights another challenge confronting Argentina: continued weaknesses in the implementation of rules surrounding competition, regulation, and the oversight of domestic markets. Because Argentina's ambitious program of structural reforms was launched simultaneously with the Convertibility Plan and within a very compressed time frame, policymakers still have some catching up to do in the areas of regulation and oversight. In some sectors, such as gas and electricity, highly professional regulatory bodies have effectively upheld the rules concerning the quality and price competitiveness of private service delivery. Yet in other sectors, such as telecommunications and water, the largest firms operating in these markets have easily captured regulatory commissions.

A more troublesome trend has been the numerous corruption scandals that have erupted around the Menem administration in the past decade, most of which arose in the context of the privatization program. For example, since 1991 the prices of privatized services have increased 55 percent more than those of other goods, a trend for which government officials have yet to offer any rational justification.[24] Trends such as these, combined with the Menem administration's excessive identification with wealthy interests and seeming indifference to heightened unemployment and distributional stress, have taken a toll on public support for market reform in Argentina. The most recent opinion polls show, for example, that just 53 percent of those interviewed consider market reform to be the country's best option, compared to a 65 percent endorsement of market reform within Latin America as a whole.[25] The deeper problem, obviously, was the Menem team's failure to implement market incentives in areas that offer the broadest efficiency and income gains (for example, labor markets and competition policy), while doggedly adhering to highly orthodox fiscal and monetary policies that work in the opposite direction.

Finally, underpinning the macro- and microeconomic trends reviewed in this chapter is the absence of a coherent development strategy to steer the political economy into the longer term. By definition, the Convertibility Plan and broader set of structural reforms based on liberalization, privatization, and deregulation signal Argentina's commitment to an outward-oriented development strategy. Such a strategy is very much in line with current thinking, which holds that the quickest way to improve a given country's level of development is through the generation of higher value added economic activities led by exports.[26] For example, it is the explicit embracement of this approach, combined with the adoption of a downwardly flexible exchange rate regime in the early 1980s, that accounts for Chile's comparative success (see table 5-4); similarly, Mexico, by aggressively promoting higher value added exports in conjunction with a floating exchange rate post-1994, is now following closely in Chile's footsteps. In both cases, increasing levels of trade have driven economic growth and investment based on higher value added activities.

Argentina does not appear to be poised for this same kind of dynamic takeoff. Although the volume of trade as a percentage of GDP has doubled since 1990, the export of low value added agricultural and energy products and the import of consumer durables and capital goods have dominated the bulk of this commercial expansion. To date, trade within Mercosur has been dominated by just two partners (Argentina and Brazil) and one sector (autos), which impedes this venue as a source of more dynamic employment expansion and export-led growth for Argentina. Again, Brazil's recent devaluation and massive adjustment have tapped into this very weakness: overnight, Argentine auto production was reduced by half. For Argentine policymakers, who continue to rule out real currency devaluation as an option, the writing is clearly on the wall; the task ahead is to deliver quickly on a set of competitive policies that, at a minimum, would reduce business costs, target higher value added exports for expansion, and better equip workers to compete in the country's rapidly changing labor markets. In the absence of a more aggressive strategy along these lines, the goals of adjusting relative prices and triggering higher growth, employment, and income gains will continue to elude Argentine policymakers.

Political Development in the Convertibility Era

Just as the launch of the Convertibility Plan put an end to years of economic chaos in Argentina, it also provided an opportunity for domestic politics to stabilize. Throughout the postwar period, economic trends had been driven largely by domestic politics, which swung erratically between military and civilian rule. The advent of the Menem administration marked the end of a long zero-sum stalemate for Argentina and the beginning of a more constructive interplay between politics and economics. Menem's election in 1989 was doubly significant in that, for the first time, a democratically elected president from one political party in Argentina passed the torch to a democratically elected president from another party. However, almost immediately, the exigencies of hyperinflation threatened to erode whatever political capital this democratic transition may have afforded. From the standpoint of politics, the country's ability to traverse the series of economic obstacles reviewed in this chapter can be broken down into three phases.

Political development during the first Menem administration (1989–95) focused single-mindedly on economic stabilization, the legislation and implementation of market reforms, and the formation of a coalition to support these policies. Similar to other market reformers in the 1990s, the government moved in autocratic fashion, passing most reforms through a flurry of executive decrees (more than twelve thousand decrees had been passed as of December 1993). But the president's own proven leadership skills also helped to rally a coalition that actively supported macroeconomic stabilization and the sustainability of the Convertibility Plan. In this respect, Menem moved masterfully, convincing potential business, labor, and middle-class allies of their future gains under a market model, while also mitigating opposition through the administration of numerous forms of direct and indirect compensation.[27] At the same time, the president and his coalition succeeded in downplaying the inevitable losses that would register at the level of the real economy, thus rendering the politics of reform at this early stage relatively straightforward: the measures may have inflicted widespread economic pain, but the initial gains in terms of inflation reduction and the resumption of growth were also perceived as broadly shared.

Thus at least from the standpoint of macroeconomic stabilization, the Menem team had mobilized sufficient support to overcome collective action dilemmas that had long plagued the country. However, as mentioned earlier, opposition to market reforms was further neutralized in ways that quickly came back to haunt policymakers, as both organized labor and the provincial governments were basically spared the same degree of liberalization and cost-cutting measures that were readily applied to most other economic sectors. While effective for retaining the support of workers and regional voters, which was crucial to the president's reelection ambitions, the Menem team's soft-pedaling of market measures in these areas quickly constituted reform gaps that would have to be bridged in order for the Convertibility Plan to succeed. Whereas the tequila shock of 1995 forced a major fiscal adjustment on the provinces, under strong pressure from the multilateral lenders, the task of passing a comprehensive labor market reform package was ultimately left to Menem's successor.

Since the reinstatement of regional governments with the return to civilian rule in 1983, Argentina has ranked next to Brazil in its high percentage of automatic fiscal transfers to the provinces and the wide spending discretion enjoyed by officials at the subnational level.[28] This fiscal arrangement between the central government and the provinces was also at the heart of executive-legislative relations in the Argentina of the 1990s, as the Peronist-controlled provinces elected the upper chamber of the legislature and were instrumental in delivering Menem's presidential victory in 1989. Apart from delaying budget cuts and the privatization of provincial banks and other public entities, the Menem administration repaid this loyalty through the negotiation of fiscal pacts in 1992 and 1993 that replaced "the distributional criteria legislated in the 1987 revenue sharing law with criteria that reflected little other than political deal making."[29] The result was a steady flow of highly discretionary fiscal transfers to the provinces, in contrast to the steep budget cuts executed in the country's urban centers. Even after the ax fell on provincial finances after 1995, the Peronist bloc in Congress succeeded in extending the discretionary nature of provincial fiscal transfers through Menem's second term, despite the opposition's demands for greater transparency and accountability.

On the labor front, although the country's business environment had been greatly transformed over the postwar period, the prevailing labor legislation dated back to the height of Peronist populism in the 1950s. For example, one large labor confederation still predominated in the negotiation of rules and salaries across entire industries and, in the event that business and labor could not agree on a new contract, the standing law held that the old contract would automatically prevail.[30] While this was hardly a recipe for the kinds of flexibility and innovation now demanded by the new market model, Menem and his congressional allies avoided direct confrontation with organized workers over labor market deregulation and other painful public sector reforms. The result was labor loyalty at the polls and a steep reduction in the number of general strikes and union mobilizations during Menem's first term, but also a series of piecemeal reforms that failed to reduce economic uncertainty or the high costs of doing business in Argentina. By 1995, the minister of labor admitted that just 30 percent of the proposed measures to modernize business-labor relations in Argentina had been implemented.[31]

With the 1995 tequila shock and Menem's reelection shortly thereafter, the politics of market reform shifted onto another plane. In the wake of the 1995 crisis, the Convertibility Plan's initial success at macroeconomic stabilization became overshadowed by the pressing need to improve the country's competitiveness under a fixed exchange rate regime and by the increasing levels of adjustment stress apparent in the figures in table 5-4. In short order, the populace's fear of skyrocketing unemployment eclipsed its fear of hyperinflation, with policymakers' heightened emphasis on promoting efficiency and productivity further fueling these insecurities. The political winds reversed, and the web of alliances that formed the pro-stabilization coalition during Menem's first term faltered in the face of these more complicated micro-level challenges. A new coalition of opposition parties pulled together and began to question the government's strategy of market reform with few safety nets. However, opposition politicians had already criticized the currency board during the 1995 presidential campaign, and they had been penalized for it at the polls. Thus, rather than tackling the Convertibility Plan head on, they began to work around its margins, taking up with a vengeance the causes of social adjustment, corruption, and judiciary reform.

It was a platform that resonated well with voters. The centrist Radical Party beat the Peronists in the first open elections for the mayor of Buenos

Aires in 1996, and in 1997 an ascendant coalition between the Radicals and center-left Frepaso bloc went on to capture a majority position in the lower house of the Chamber of Deputies. The message at this point was twofold: Argentine voters were spooked by the tequila shock but still not prepared to abandon a strategy that had finally purged the country of hyperinflation; yet the sacrifices inflicted by market adjustment had also invoked an adamantly distributional response at the polls, including in the provinces, where the Peronists retained their majority hold on state governorships but lost an increasing percentage of the popular vote. The legacy of the tequila shock was such that the losers in the reform process were now reluctant to bear the burden of further adjustment, even though a long list of deregulatory and efficiency-enhancing measures had yet to be tackled. In contrast to Menem's first term, the politics of market reform after 1995 were anything but straightforward and the solutions on the distributional front had become more complex.

At this juncture in the reform process, it had also become clear that a currency board that restrains a government from reckless policies in one area could work unwittingly to prohibit the pursuit of sensible policies in another. A major dilemma was that the kinds of competitive measures now necessary to render the Convertibility Plan viable offered gains that were more subtle and dispersed (efficiency, productivity), while the pain of adjustment (unemployment, bankruptcy) was more concentrated. As the economic landscape during Menem's second term became more deflationary and volatile, with annual growth bouncing from –4.6 percent in 1995 to 8.4 percent in 1997 and back down to –3.2 percent in 1999, those coalitional bases that had supported the first phase of economic stabilization further deteriorated. The opposition victories of 1996–97 had driven home the fact that a currency board arrangement may actually require greater and more sophisticated political management in order to deepen and sustain the ruling coalition under inevitably changing economic circumstances. But by now the damage had been done, as the electoral losses had triggered a premature succession battle within the Peronist ranks.

As government leadership waned, little was actually accomplished in the way of continuing market reform during Menem's second term. This was made all the more apparent when, in the midst of 1999's steep recession within the real economy, it was the government that dropped the ball in seeking viable solutions. Fearful of adding to the already high level of adjustment stress and mired in internal party politics, the best the Menem administration could manage was to pass a labor reform law that pleased no one. The law basically condoned a dual labor market, leaving some workers highly protected and others to fend for themselves. Labor was dissatisfied with the law's all-or-nothing character, and the private sector objected on the grounds that the law did not go far enough in guaranteeing lower costs for business. As it turned out, this collective action stand-off was resolved a year later by Menem's successors, but it again highlighted the challenges that countries across the region must grapple with as political and economic leaders seek to deepen the market reforms now in place.

One positive outcome of the Brazilian devaluation and ensuing recession was that both labor and domestic producers in Argentina signaled a greater willingness to cooperate in the design of policies to promote competitiveness. Organized labor responded to its frustration with the second Menem administration and its marketplace losses in two major ways. Those factions that were most affected by layoffs and company retrenchment became increasingly vocal in demanding more adequate levels of adjustment assistance. Yet a sizable segment of organized labor also sought to adapt to market restructuring by bargaining over flexibility and productivity criteria and through participation in such privatization-related activities as employee ownership and stock options.[32] For their part, domestic producers reaffirmed their allegiance to the currency board, at the same time turning up the heat on policymakers to take stronger action in reducing high business costs and easing the flow of affordable credit to the private sector.[33] The inability of the outgoing Menem administration to orchestrate a more effective set of policy responses suggested that, regardless of party affiliation, it was time to pass the torch to a new reform coalition.

Which brings us to the third political phase: the October 1999 presidential election and its aftermath.[34] To the surprise of few, the election was handily won by Buenos Aires mayor Fernando de la Rúa, who took almost 50 percent of the popular vote as the candidate of the Radical Party–Frepaso Alliance (Alianza Democrática). The losers in the presidential race, Peronist candidate Eduardo Duhalde and former finance minister Domingo Cavallo, took 38 percent and 10 percent of the vote, respectively. Ironically, the only candidate that hinted at changing significantly the policies that support the currency board was the Peronist candidate, who based his campaign simultaneously on the laurels of the Convertibility Plan and the Justicialista Party's role in launching it. Although Duhalde's ambiguous campaign rhetoric—including a short-lived proposal for a moratorium on Argentina's external debt service payments and a return to higher levels of corporatism and trade protection—did little to endear him to voters or the international financial community, the Peronist loss of the presidency was part and parcel of the political economic trajectory that had been under way since the 1997 midterm elections.

In short, intense Peronist party infighting, including Menem's failed effort to reverse a constitutional ban against running for a third consecutive term and the black cloud of corruption and insensitivity to social hardship that increasingly surrounded Menem's administration, was ultimately Duhalde's undoing at the polls. While Cavallo's pledges of anticorruption and the deepening of administrative reform were far more credible than the "robber baron" image of the Peronists, as the official architect of the Convertibility Plan, he too suffered the reputation of not caring enough about social issues. By contrast, de la Rúa persevered with the same message that had produced opposition victories from 1996 on: continuation of the Convertibility Plan and the fundamental fiscal and monetary policies necessary to support it, but also commitment to forge ahead more aggressively in fine-tuning the prevailing economic model on the social front. Specifically, the incoming president pledged to fight unemployment by providing greater adjustment relief (for example, subsidizing debt interest payments) for those small- and medium-size firms that account for the bulk of Argentine jobs, and to cut the fiscal deficit in ways that did not depend strictly on further austerity (for example, by cracking down harder on tax evaders, and through the elimination of government waste and graft).[35]

Turn-of-the-century politics in Argentina reflect, first, that the country has come a very long way toward resolving the kinds of zero-sum outcomes that characterized the pre-reform period; and, second, that the Menem administration's earlier strategy of protecting illiberal enclaves, negotiating deals that were untenable in the long run, and holding the losers from market reform at arm's length had simply run its course. Now, in the wake of the Brazilian shock, a new economic team faces the challenges of charting a course of sustainable growth, exhibiting savvy external debt management, and increasing the country's productivity levels and overall competitiveness. Somewhere along the way, the de la Rúa administration is also going to have to articulate a development strategy proper that can steer the economic model in the direction of higher value added exports and much more dynamic job creation.

These necessities alone are enough to shorten any political honeymoon, and the Peronists' continued control of the provinces, the Federal Senate, and the Supreme Court could short-circuit it all the more. On the other hand, the Peronist opposition already has its eye on recapturing the presidency, and hence has a vested interest in cooperating on political economic initiatives that will bolster the prevailing model.[36] This is evident, for example, in the broad congressional support that de la Rúa has already garnered in the areas of tax reform, cost cutting (for example, reducing prices on fuel, highway tolls, and railroad freight), and further public sector downsizing.

Tellingly, the new administration has also advanced in reforming those sectors in which the Peronists may have been politically beholden, but the Alianza is not. For example, revenue flows to at least five bankrupt provinces have been cut, imposing greater fiscal responsibility at the subnational level, and a comprehensive labor bill was finally passed during the first six months of de la Rúa's term. The new labor code decentralizes contract negotiations so that differences in company size and changing sectoral demands are better accommodated and encourages businesses to hire more workers at lower costs. On this count, the payroll tax on new hires was reduced from 17.5 percent to 12 percent, and good-faith bargaining on both sides is now encouraged by the elimination of the rule that retained old contracts in the event that negotiations over a new agreement failed.[37]

The ultimate fate of the Convertibility Plan depends entirely on what further progress is made in tackling this more difficult set of "second-generation" market reforms. The tasks at hand are more than just technical exercises. Now, further progress with market reforms will require wider participation and good-faith negotiation with those most affected, on complex issues ranging from additional tax and cost reductions to the more vigorous implementation of rules surrounding regulation, transparency, and oversight. What is at stake is the de la Rúa administration's ability to persevere in assertively overcoming those collective action obstacles that have deterred policymakers and political leaders from tackling the remaining barriers to productivity, efficiency, and greater equity in the Argentine economy.

Conclusion

This chapter began by asking why Argentina has stayed with a fixed rate currency regime when all of its emerging-market neighbors have moved toward exchange rate flexibility. As is usually the case with such matters, the question is much simpler than the answer. The track record over the past decade shows that the original decision to fix the peso to the U.S. dollar was a sound one, given Argentina's complete loss of credibility by 1991.

However, as the analysis also shows, the economic conditions that under-pin the currency board have changed markedly over time. By implementing an ambitious set of market reforms in conjunction with the Convertibility Plan, Argentina has dramatically increased its level of economic openness as well as its exposure to high levels of external debt and international capital mobility in the 1990s.

The experience of the three other countries in this book has been one of increased exchange rate flexibility to better facilitate adjustment and mitigate the potentially harsh impact of international volatility. Argentina's resistance to this same transition is perhaps best understood in the context of the domestic political economy. Sustained periods of economic growth and prosperity have proved elusive in Argentina, particularly compared with the other countries analyzed in this volume. The hyperinflation of the more recent past was a last straw of sorts, leaving policymakers and the public at large extremely reluctant to venture from a fixed exchange rate that finally stabilized the economy. Yet in light of Mexico's rapid recovery under a floating exchange rate since 1995 and Brazil's unexpectedly early turnaround after moving to a similar currency regime in early 1999, there is an outside chance that history is repeating itself. By purposefully tying their hands to a currency board, Argentine policymakers have relinquished the most basic monetary and fiscal tools that have helped spur economic recovery in these other countries. The currency board's future may be sound, but the credibility of the Argentine reform program will suffer if the country continues to rely on highly recessionary measures and excessive external borrowing just to guarantee its survival.

What lessons might the Argentine case offer for debates over fixed versus flexible exchange rates? First, it appears that maintaining a strong currency does not necessarily mean having a strong economy. As this analysis has shown, despite the supposed invincibility of the Convertibility Plan and the heroic advances in the way of fiscal discipline and deep financial sector reform, the Argentine economy is still fraught with numerous weaknesses related to efficiency, productivity, and trade competitiveness. A second lesson, moreover, is that the credibility of a given reform program can be a moving target—especially in a world of high capital mobility. It is questionable, for example, whether the Menem administration's commitment to "dollarize before devaluing" enhanced its credibility. If anything, this gesture cast an even stronger international spotlight on the frailties of the Argentine economy, thus prompting the need for higher domestic interest rates and further borrowing to bolster credibility.

Finally, as Timothy Kessler and Eliana Cardoso both pointed out in their chapters, well-rehearsed arguments in pre-devaluation Mexico and Brazil about how rapid productivity gains in the tradable goods sector would compensate for real exchange rate appreciation simply never panned out. Instead, as Cardoso notes, "the government's self-deception entail[ed] an increasingly expensive commitment to guarantee an untenable outcome." As the de la Rúa administration continues to pledge its full allegiance to the Convertibility Plan, it remains to be seen if Argentina will be able to beat these difficult odds. At the very least, policymakers and legislators appear to have picked up the pace in launching the kinds of policies that will be essential for strengthening market confidence and improving competitiveness.

In terms of the political economy of market reform in Argentina, it is worth reiterating two other lessons from the Menem era. First, despite the apparent simplicity of the currency board, and the hands-off management style that it implies, the same cannot be said of the political strategies necessary to support it. If anything, a fixed exchange rate has created ever greater pressures for more flexible and intensive political management, as domestic actors have been forced to adjust to the demands imposed by the Convertibility Plan.

Second, electoral trends since 1996 confirm that a political coalition to support micro-level restructuring in Argentina does not flow naturally from the same alliances that fostered macroeconomic stabilization and the launching of fundamental market reforms (liberalization, privatization, deregulation). The kind of grand electoral alliance that enabled the Radical-Frepaso coalition to capture the presidency is perhaps best seen as an interim political strategy in grappling with this challenge. While not beholden to the same labor and provincial interests that obstructed the full implementation of the Peronist reform package, the de la Rúa administration faces challenges to its ability to govern by virtue of the very diverse claims that back it.[38] Although the Alianza Democrática is off to a good start, the difficult but not impossible task of cementing a political coalition to tackle the full range of micro-level reforms still lies ahead.

Notes

1. Francesco Caramazza and Jahangir Aziz, *Fixed or Flexible? Getting the Exchange Rate Right in the 1990s* (International Monetary Fund, 1998), pp. 16–17.

2. On the role of flexible exchange rates in the Washington reform package, see John Williamson, "The Progress of Policy Reform in Latin America," in John Williamson, ed., *Latin American Adjustment: How Much Has Happened?* (Institute for International Economics, 1989), pp. 369–72.

3. These debates are reviewed in W. Max Corden, *Economic Policy, Exchange Rates, and the International System* (University of Chicago Press, 1994); Ricardo Hausmann and others, "The Exchange Rate Debate," *Latin American Economic Policies*, vol. 7 (second quarter 1999), pp. 1–10; and Richard J. Sweeney, Clas G. Wihlbor, and Thomas D. Willett, eds., *Exchange Rate Policies for Emerging Market Economies* (Boulder: Westview Press, 1999).

4. A full discussion of the pros and cons of currency boards can be found in Steve Hanke and Kurt Shuler, "Currency Boards and Currency Convertibility," *Cato Journal*, vol. 12 (1993), pp. 687–705; John Williamson, *What Role for Currency Boards?* (Institute for International Economics, 1995); and Richard J. Sweeney, "Exchange Rate Crises: Are Currency Boards the Answer for Emerging Market Economies?" in Sweeney, Wihlbor, and Willett, eds., *Exchange Rate Policies*, pp. 265–94.

5. Caramazza and Aziz, *Fixed or Flexible?* p. 7.

6. Ibid., p. 5.

7. The arguments in this section borrow from those developed by Manuel Pastor and Carol Wise in two articles: "Stabilization and Its Discontents: Argentina's Economic Restructuring in the 1990's," *World Development*, vol. 27 (1999), pp. 477–503; and "The Politics of Second-Generation Reform," *Journal of Democracy*, vol. 10 (1999), pp. 34–48.

8. I. M. D. Little, Richard N. Cooper, W. Max Corden, and Sarath Rajapatirana, *Boom, Crisis, and Adjustment: The Macroeconomic Experience of Developing Countries* (New York: Oxford University Press and the World Bank, 1993), pp. 185–92.

9. Pablo Gerchunoff and Juan Carlos Torre, "La política de liberalización económica en la administración de Menem," *Desarrollo Económico*, vol. 36 (October–December 1996), pp. 733–68.

10. Fundación de Investigaciones Económicas Latinoamericanas (FIEL), "A Special Report on the Argentine Economy during 1991–1995," *Indicadores de Coyuntura*, vol. 350 (October 1995), pp. iii–xviii.

11. Pamela K. Starr, "Government Coalitions and the Viability of Currency Boards: Argentina under the Cavallo Plan," *Journal of Interamerican Studies and World Affairs*, vol. 39 (1997), pp. 83–133.

12. All dollar amounts are U.S. dollars.

13. FIEL, "Argentine Economy," p. xv; and Gerchunoff and Torre, "La política de liberalización económica," p. 129.

14. Little, Cooper, Corden, and Rajapatirana, *Boom, Crisis, and Adjustment*, p. 194.

15. See Javier Corrales, "Presidents, Ruling Parties, and Party Rules: A Theory on the Politics of Economic Reform in Latin America," *Comparative Politics*, vol. 32 (2000), pp. 127–50; and Juliana Bambaci, Tamara Saront, and Mariano Tommasi, "The Political Economy of Economic Reforms in Argentina," Centro de Estudios para el Desarrollo Institucional (CEDI), Buenos Aires, January 2000.

16. Economist Intelligence Unit, "Argentina," Country Report, 4th quarter 1998 (London), p. 8; and Charles Calomiris, "A Welcome to Foreign Banks Could Energize Mexico," *Wall Street Journal*, July 16, 1999, p. A15.

17. J. P. Morgan, "Monetary Union in the Americas," *Economic Research Note* (February 12, 1999).

18. Clifford Kraus, "Argentines Suffering from Brazil Crisis," *New York Times*, February 8, 1999, p. A8.

19. "Focus on Big Financial Challenge," *Latin American Weekly Report*, November 30, 1999, pp. 42–43.

20. Carolina Pessino, "The Labor Market during the Transition in Argentina," in Sebastian Edwards and Nora Lustig, eds., *Labor Market Reform in Latin America* (Brookings, 1997), pp. 151–200. Others have argued that because of the slow progress in reforming labor markets, and the cumulative toll that an uncompetitive exchange rate has taken in perpetuating high unemployment, making labor codes more flexible will matter little if relative prices remain distorted. See Alejandro B. Rofman, *Convertibilidad y desocupación en la Argentina de los '90* (University of Buenos Aires, 1997).

21. Nancy Birdsall and Juan Luis Londono, "Asset Inequality Matters," *American Economic Review,* vol. 87 (1997), pp. 32–38.

22. Daniel Azpiazu, *La concentración en la industria argentina a mediados de los años noventa* (Buenos Aires: FLACSO, 1998).

23. "Argentina's Drift toward Concentration," *Latin American Weekly Report*, October 5, 1995.

24. "Argentina's Economy: Keeping the Reform Alive," *Economist*, October 23, 1999, p. 26.

25. The poll, based on face-to-face interviews with 14,839 adults in urban areas in Latin America, was conducted by Latinobarómetro in December 1998 and January 1999.

26. Sebastian Edwards, "Latin America's Underperformance," *Foreign Affairs,* vol. 76 (March–April 1997), pp. 93–103.

27. See Sebastian Edwards and Daniel Lederman, "The Political Economy of Unilateral Trade Liberalization: The Case of Chile," Working Paper 6510 (Cambridge, Mass.: National Bureau of Economic Research, April 1998), p. 62, table 5. According to Edwards and Lederman, direct compensation consists of the transfer of cash or securities to groups adversely affected by a given reform; indirect compensation "implies compensating groups affected by a particular reform through the adjustment of a different policy that indirectly raises their revenues or reduces their costs of production." There is ample evidence that the Menem reform strategy depended heavily on such compensatory mechanisms, as suggested by Vicente Palermo and Marcos Novaro, *Política y poder en el gobierno de Menem* (Buenos Aires: Grupo Editorial Norma, 1996).

28. This summary of the political ties between the central government and the provinces borrows from Kathleen O'Neill, "Tugging at the Purse Strings: Fiscal Decentralization and State Discretion," paper presented at the annual meeting of the Latin American Studies Association, Miami, March 2000, pp. 9–11.

29. Kent Eaton, "Political Obstacles to Decentralization in Argentina and the Philippines," paper presented at the annual meeting of the American Political Science Association, Boston, Mass., September 1998, p. 7 (cited in O'Neill, "Tugging at the Purse Strings," p. 11).

30. Clifford Krauss, "Injecting Change into Argentina," *New York Times*, March 8, 2000, p. C1.

31. Cited in Bambaci, Saront, and Tommasi, "Economic Reforms in Argentina," p. 17.

32. M. Victoria Murillo, "Union Politics, Market-Oriented Reforms, and the Reshaping of Argentine Corporatism," in Douglas Chalmers and others, *The New Politics of Inequality in Latin America* (Oxford University Press, 1997), pp. 72–94.

33. Ken Warn, "Presidential Initiative Pays Off: Argentina," *Financial Times*, March 12, 1999, p. 5.

34. For more detail on the 1999 presidential race, see William C. Smith, "The End of the Menem Era in Argentina," *North-South Center Update*, October 25, 1999.

35. See ibid. and "Argentina's Economy," 23–26.

36. William Perry, "Argentina Faces the Future," *Hemisphere 2000*, March 15, 2000, p. 1.

37. See J. P. Morgan, "Data Watch: Argentina," *Global Data Watch*, April 28, 2000, p. 29.

38. Comments by Juan Corradi at a workshop on "Post-Reform Elections in Latin America," School of Advanced International Studies (SAIS), Johns Hopkins University, Washington, D.C., March 4, 2000.

6

JAVIER CORRALES

Reform-Lagging States and the Question of Devaluation:

Venezuela's Response to the Exogenous Shocks of 1997–98

IT IS NOT UNUSUAL for developing countries to respond to external economic shocks by refusing to devalue their currencies. This response, many economists argue, is fraught with huge costs and risks. It is costly because it leads to an overvaluation of the currency, a blow to export diversification, and a sharp deterioration in employment. It is risky because defending an already overvalued currency in the midst of macroeconomic imbalances often fails, leading to a devaluation that is far greater than expected.[1] Moreover it is defiant, because it goes against the advice of politically powerful policy experts, including officials from the International Monetary Fund (IMF), who invariably recommend a devaluation combined with structural reforms. And yet numerous developing countries respond to external shocks by defending, rather than devaluing, their currencies.[2] Why are so many developing countries attracted to a policy of currency defense despite these costs, risks, and advice? To identify the reasons for this choice, this chapter reviews the case of Venezuela, which responded to exogenous shocks of 1997–98 by refusing to devalue.

I am grateful to Roberto Bottome, Delia Boylan, Imelda Cisneros, Jorge I. Domínguez, Jeanne K. Giraldo, Janet Kelly, Moritz Kraemer, Manuel Lago, James Mahon, Pedro Palma, Abdón Suzzarini, Germán Utreras, Beth Yarbrough, and the contributors to this volume for their comments.

Since the mid-1980s, Venezuela has experienced several "start-and-stop" reform cycles. Each new administration launches a program of economic reforms, only to relax it prematurely, culminating in a deep economic crisis. Venezuela is thus a quintessential reform-lagging state. By the end of the 1990s, Venezuela had yet to consolidate a complete package of first-generation market reforms, setting it apart from most major Latin American countries, which made impressive strides in reforming their economies throughout the 1990s.[3]

It was in this reform-lagging context that Venezuela experienced one of its most severe economic shocks of the last fifteen years. Many experts and pressure groups, including the powerful state oil company, Petróleos de Venezuela, S.A. (PDVSA), called for a major devaluation together with a package of fiscal adjustments and microeconomic reforms. The Venezuelan government chose instead to defend the overvalued bolivar, raise interest rates, and burn reserves. In short, the Venezuelan state responded by tightening, rather than relaxing, its already restrictive monetary policy and inflexible exchange rate regime.[4] Government officials understood the costs and risks associated with this choice. They had only to look at their own country's history to realize that resisting devaluation pressures often proves counterproductive. So why did Venezuelan officials follow the same path again? More generally, why do economically battered countries respond to external shocks by trying to uphold a fixed or tightly managed exchange rate regime?

This chapter argues that the answer lies in domestic politics in general, and state-based variables in particular. When reform-lagging countries experience exogenous shocks, defending a tight exchange rate regime emerges as a politically promising response, or rather, as the most viable political response available to the state. The inability to consolidate economic reforms leaves the state with very few policy instruments with which to respond to shocks when they occur. Most state institutions are in disarray and unable to deliver credible responses. As Stephan Haggard argued in his discussion of the choice of development models in postwar East Asia and Latin America, states respond to economic imperatives not necessarily by implementing what is economically optimal, but what is feasible within "the range of policy instruments that the state commands."[5] Venezuelan government officials realized that the IMF prescription of devaluation plus structural reforms was impractical, not because it was economically unsound—rather the reverse—but because the state could not deliver it. The state faced a crisis of credibility. Its hands were tied by pressure groups and political parties. The only state institution immune to this crisis of credibility and paralysis, government officials reasoned, was the central bank. Hence the central bank was given full rein to handle the crisis. And the central bank did what central banks do best: it deployed restrictive monetary and stabilizing exchange rate policies. The Venezuelan state thus responded by exploiting its own institutional advantage, that is, by relying on the central bank despite societal pressures to the contrary.

This chapter also shows that governments conduct more than just a narrow cost-benefit analysis when designing exchange rate policy. Venezuelan authorities had two other considerations in mind. One was the need to signal credibility. They chose the exchange rate for this purpose since it is one of the most visible and highly watched prices in any developing economy—an ideal signaling device. The other consideration was an estimate of the probability of failure. The government knew that either policy, devaluing or defending, could result in a nightmarish scenario, namely, a failure to convince speculators, which could ultimately lead to a maxidevaluation. Yet the government estimated that defending the bolivar had a lower probability of producing this outcome than engaging in a managed devaluation. This is because policymakers realized that the central bank was the only state agency capable of adhering to a chosen policy path despite societal pressures. By placing all its bets on the central bank, the government was no doubt taking a gamble, but one that was informed by a reasonable assessment of institutional strengths.

The surprise of the Venezuelan story is that the state achieved its intended objectives. The central bank defeated one of the most serious currency crises in Latin America, avoiding a maxidevaluation. Few countries with economic fundamentals as poor as those of Venezuela in 1998 achieved this. Colombia, Ecuador, and Brazil tried but failed. This chapter also seeks to explain Venezuela's relative success in keeping the lid on a potential currency crisis, arguing that this outcome had less to do with the level of reserves than with the level of resolve.

Finally, this chapter reiterates the perils of being a reform-lagging country in the era of globalization. Some political economists have argued that the implementation of market-oriented reforms, which exposes nations to greater competition and volatile capital flows, restricts the capacity of states to manage economic affairs. In contrast, this chapter argues that being a reform-lagging state is far more restrictive. Venezuela's inability to consolidate a program of necessary reforms rendered the country more vulnerable to external shocks, more constrained in its policy response, and more prone to pursue economic policies that were much more costly in the end.

The Three Shocks of 1997–98

What kinds of shocks can rattle an emerging market? The answer, analysts typically suggest, is an international financial crisis, a precipitous drop in the price of a country's main exports, or a rise in domestic political uncertainty. If sufficiently severe, any such shock can wreak havoc on currency markets, possibly plunging a country into a deep economic crisis. Venezuela in 1998 experienced all three shocks intensely and simultaneously. The result was, predictably, a series of financial panics that led to one of the most serious economic recessions ever, one of Latin America's worst economic performances for the year, and the collapse of a thirty-year-old political party system.

The first external shock stemmed from the Asian financial crisis that began to unfold in the second half of 1997. This crisis produced a slowdown in the world's real GDP, from 4.2 percent in 1997 to 2.5 percent in 1998, a decline in world trade growth from 9.9 percent to 3.6 percent, and a complete panic in international financial markets.[6] As capital markets contracted, investors quickly fled from the more economically fragile emerging markets, which led to speculative attacks on a number of currencies. When Russia was forced to devalue and then to default on its outstanding debts, international panic escalated. Venezuela, which had attracted significant foreign investments after 1996 due to the launch that year of a program of market reforms called "Agenda Venezuela," became the next target of capital flight.

The second and most important economic shock was a precipitous decline in the price of oil. Venezuela is one of the most important exporters of oil in the world, a founding member of the Organization of Petroleum Exporting Countries (OPEC), and a leading supplier of oil to the United States. In 1997 oil provided Venezuela with 80 percent of its export revenues and more than 60 percent of its fiscal revenues.[7] One consequence of the Asian crisis was to reduce world demand for oil. In addition, OPEC decided to increase oil production at the end of 1997. Although OPEC (and Mexico, Norway, and Egypt) made cutbacks in 1998, these were offset by the decision of the United Nations to allow Iraq to raise its production ceiling. The result was an underdemand and an oversupply of oil that depressed its price throughout 1998 (see table 6-1). Whereas Venezuela's 1998 budget was originally calculated on the assumption of an average oil price of $15.50 a barrel, the actual price by the end of 1998 was closer to $9.65 a barrel, the lowest in more than two decades. Oil prices recovered handsomely in 1999, so that it is hard to remember the almost 37 percent decline in oil prices in 1997–98. But though short-lived, this decline was severe: it practically decimated Venezuela's fiscal revenues in 1998–99.

The third shock was a rise in political risk caused by unusually high levels of electoral uncertainty. Starting in April 1998, public opinion polls revealed that the winner in the upcoming December presidential election would most likely be Hugo Chávez Frías, the candidate with the most antagonistic views toward market reforms. Unknown to Venezuelans before 1992, Chávez became politically prominent when he led an unsuccessful coup in February 1992 against the Carlos Andrés Pérez administration (1989–93), one of the most market-oriented governments ever in Venezuela. Throughout 1998 Chávez conducted a highly populist and nationalistic campaign peppered with repeated attacks against "savage capitalism." He criticized crucial privatizations such as those in the aluminum and iron sectors, and he engaged in a vindictive antiestablishment discourse.[8] He talked about carrying out a "revolution" that, however "peaceful," would punish those found guilty of corruption. Economic agents panicked.[9] Three scenarios seemed possible, each as worrisome as the others—a coup to prevent a Chávez victory, a massive Chávez-led upheaval if he lost the elections, or a wrecked economy and political disorder if he won the elections.

The first casualty of these shocks was the Caracas stock exchange, which dropped by more than half between September 1997 and June 1998.[10] The drop precipitated a speculative attack against the bolivar in May 1998. The government restructured the budget to reflect the new lower price of oil, for a total nominal decrease in spending of 5.9 percent. The combination of capital flight and lower spending unleashed a severe economic recession in the second semester of 1998, which was especially onerous for the manufacturing sector (see table 6-1).

This recession, however, was only the beginning. By August 1998, shortly after the Russian debacle, investors made a second and more unsettling run on the bolivar. For many outside investors, Venezuela looked too much like Russia: oil exports were dominant, economic reforms were stalled, and antimarket political forces were gaining strength. Expectations of an impending devaluation of the bolivar mounted. At this point, the

Table 6-1. *Economic Indicators for Venezuela, 1998*

Month (quarter)	Oil price per barrel (U.S. $)	Reserve[a] (U.S. $ billions)	Total GDP (percentage change)	Manufacturing sector GDP (percentage change)	Real interest rate[b]	Stock market (index)[c]	Exchange rate
January	14.43				0.03	7,332.8	511.25
February	13.45				8.33	7,175.6	517.00
March (1)	12.41	−2.02	−3.82	1.29	3.22	7,658.8	525.50
April	12.97				−4.09	6,104.3	537.00
May	13.17				2.58	6,179.5	538.75
June (2)	11.70	−0.30	1.46	−0.86	29.60	4,802.6	553.50
July	11.97				41.99	4,846.4	563.25
August	12.00				35.91	2,904.0	582.50
September (3)	12.95	−2.49	−3.09	−7.42	63.19	3,893.9	574.00
October	12.51				21.52	3,506.1	568.00
November	11.08				29.52	3,944.0	572.75
December (4)	9.65	1.84	−2.96	−8.97	25.88	4,788.7	565.00

Source: *VenEconomy Monthly* (April 1999).

a. Net change from previous quarter.

b. Loans.

c. December 1993 = 100.

Venezuelan stock exchange essentially evaporated, dropping to just 2,904 points by the end of August—an almost 75 percent decline in one year.

The Venezuelan government responded by meeting fully the increase in demand for dollars. By the end of the third quarter of 1998, the central bank depleted $4.8 billion in reserves (a 27 percent drop from December 1997). In addition, the central bank deployed a highly restrictive monetary policy, increasing the yield on central bank–issued monetary stabilization bills to encourage investors not to flee the bolivar. In September the bank was offering yields in certificates of deposit of 60.1 percent for ten-day instruments, effectively killing domestic credit.

The restrictive monetary policy and quasi-fixed exchange rate succeeded in defeating the speculative attack. The bank's resilience severely hurt those agents who had borrowed bolivars domestically to buy dollars. These agents found their bolivar-denominated debts subject to very high interest rates. Soon debtors had to sell the very same dollars they had purchased in order to service their bolivar-denominated debts. By the end of September, demand for the bolivar recovered and the value of the bolivar rose to pre-crisis levels.

Although the central bank won the battle, the battlefield was left in shambles. Defending the bolivar further squeezed an already damaged economy, making Venezuela one of the worst Latin American economic performers in 1998–99 (see figures 6-1, 6-2, 6-3, and 6-4). Venezuela's economic recession deepened in the final quarter of 1998, as the fiscal deficit approached 10 percent of gross domestic product and unemployment soared to almost 21.9 percent among the young (fifteen to twenty-four years of age). Although the decline in aggregate demand and the rise in political uncertainty—more so than the central bank's policies—had caused the huge recession of 1998, the bank's tight policies hindered any prospects for a quick recovery. Yet it is clear that in the absence of these policies, Venezuela's recession would have been far more pronounced.

The Pattern of Reform in Venezuela: Ax, Relax, and Collapse

However significant, the external shocks of 1998 were not the cause of Venezuela's economic travails during 1997–99. The real cause was a more fundamental political problem: the persistent failure in the past fifteen years to consolidate a program of economic reform. This history of failed

Figure 6-1. *Public Sector Deficit or Surplus, Selected Latin American Countries, 1997–99*[a]

Percentages of GDP

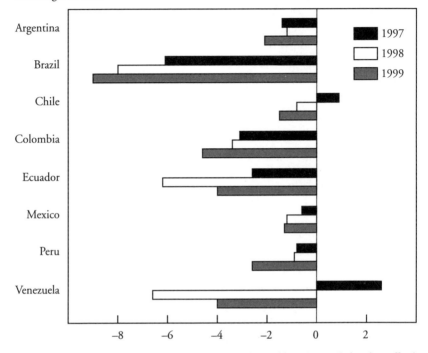

Source: Economic Commission for Latin America and the Caribbean (ECLAC), based on official figures.

a. Deficits and surpluses are calculated on the basis of local currency at current prices. Data include the nonfinancial public sector. Data for Argentina exclude provinces and municipalities. Data for Peru include the central government only. 1999 figures are preliminary estimates.

reforms explains why Venezuela was so susceptible to these shocks, and so constrained in delivering a response.

Until the mid-1970s, Venezuela was thought to be a miracle country. It had achieved industrialization, labor incorporation, and dramatic improvements in living standards, all without exhibiting those vices common in Latin America, such as macroeconomic imbalances (inflation and debt were low), political instability (class and party conflicts were low), and authoritarianism (democratic parties alternated in office uninterruptedly). By the early 1980s, however, Venezuela had begun to look less like a miracle and more like the rest of Latin America. Specifically, it began to expe-

Figure 6-2. *Urban Unemployment, Selected Latin American Countries, 1997–99*[a]

Average annual rates

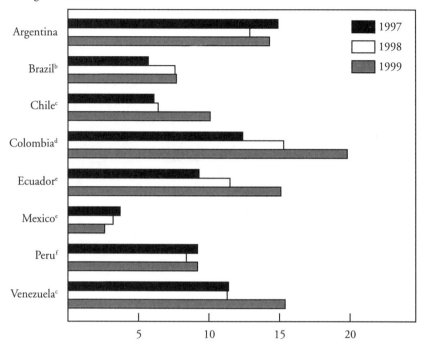

Source: See figure 6-1.

a. 1999 data are averages over January to October for Brazil; the first three quarters for Chile and Colombia; and the first six months for Peru.

b. Six metropolitan areas.

c. Total national data.

d. Seven metropolitan areas.

e. Total urban areas.

f. Metropolitan Lima.

rience chronic foreign debt, macroeconomic imbalances, exchange rate crises, repressed financial markets, erosion of democratic vitality, nonadaptation of political institutions, weakening of state structures, and growing political and societal unrest.[11]

Starting in 1979, four democratically elected administrations and one provisional government came to office with a commitment to correct these ailments. And yet Venezuela sank further into what I call an ax-relax-collapse cycle of reform. Each cycle begins with the eruption of a serious

Figure 6-3. *Consumer Prices, Selected Latin American Countries, 1997–99*[a]
December–December variations

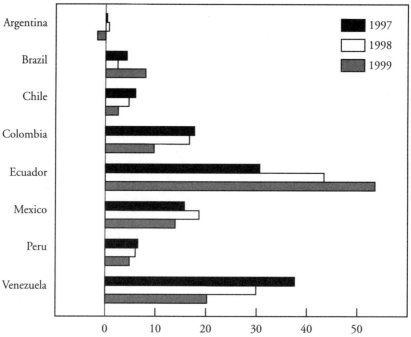

Source: See figure 6-1.
a. 1999 data represent variation from November 1998 to November 1999.

economic crisis. The government responds by implementing harsh adjustments that impose severe costs across society—the "ax." The reforms produce some results but soon lose momentum because they are either poorly
implemented or prematurely abandoned—the "relax" stage. This relaxation
culminates in yet another economic crisis—the "collapse"—setting the stage
for another round of reforms. This cycle has been repeated four times since
1979 (see table 6-2). Venezuela is thus a case, not of reform avoidance or
reform implementation, but rather of reform nonconsolidation.

    Alberto Alesina and Allan Drazen have advanced the influential argu-
ment that the repeated failure of reform efforts can work to the advantage
of the reformers, because it can lead to the attrition of reform opponents.[12]
However, in Venezuela this history of aborted reforms has complicated
rather than facilitated the prospects for economic recovery: repeated reform

Figure 6-4. *Per Capita GDP, Selected Latin American Countries, 1997–99*[a]

Percent

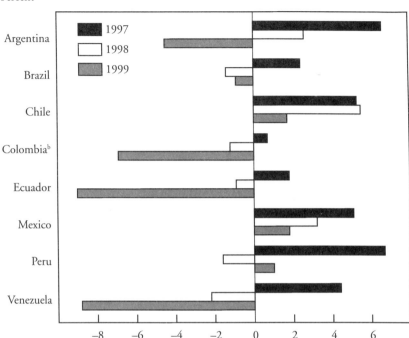

Source: See figure 6-1.

a. Calculated from local data converted into constant 1995 U.S. dollars.

b. Estimated from provisional data provided by the Colombian National Bureau of Statistics (DANE).

failures have left Venezuela with a set of unresolved problems and given rise to a new set of problems specific to reform laggards.

Unresolved Inherited Problems

Some of these problems are typical of pre-reform Latin America: chronic inflation, which did not decline below 30 percent between the late 1980s and 1997; a structural fiscal deficit, despite continuous cutbacks in spending throughout the 1990s; scanty nonoil fiscal revenues; a distorted, exemption-ridden, and chronically insufficient tax system; and ineffective and underfunded public services. Moreover, sectors such as electricity, pharmaceuticals, and agriculture were still regulated with nontransparent

Table 6-2. *The Ax-Relax-Collapse Pattern of Economic Reform in Venezuela*

Administration	Ax	Relax	Collapse
Luis Herrera Campíns (1979–84)	1979	1980–81	1983
Jaime Lusinchi (1984–89)	1983–85	1986–88	1988
Carlos A. Pérez (1989–93)			
Ramón Velásquez (1993–94)[a]	1989–91	1991–92	1993–95
Rafael Caldera (1994–99)	1996	1997	1998

Sources: For Campíns, Ricardo Hausmann and Gustavo Márquez, "La crisis económica venezolana: Origen, mecanismos y encadenamientos," *Investigación Económica*, vol. 165 (1983), pp. 117–54; and Miguel Rodríguez, "Public Sector Behavior in Venezuela," in Felipe Larraín and Marcelo Selowsky, eds., *The Public Sector and the Latin American Crisis* (San Francisco: ICS Press, 1991). For Lusinchi, Ricardo Hausmann, "Venezuela," in John Williamson, ed., *Latin American Adjustment: How Much Has Happened?* (Washington: Institute for International Economics, 1990). For Pérez and for Velásquez, Moisés Naím, *Paper Tigers and Minotaurs: The Politics of Venezuela's Economic Reforms* (Washington: Carnegie Endowment for International Peace, 1993); Javier Corrales, "Presidents, Ruling Parties, and Party Rules: A Theory on the Politics of Economic Reform in Latin America," *Comparative Politics*, vol. 32 (2000), pp. 127–50; Aníbal Romero, "Rearranging the Deck Chairs on the Titanic: The Agony of Democracy in Venezuela," *Latin American Research Review*, vol. 32, no. 1 (1997), pp. 7–36; Jennifer McCoy and William C. Smith, "From Deconsolidation to Reequilibration? Prospects for Democratic Renewal in Venezuela," in Jennifer McCoy and others, eds., *Venezuelan Democracy under Stress* (New Brunswick, N.J.: Transaction Books, 1995); and Juan Carlos Navarro, "Reversal of Fortune: The Ephemeral Success of Adjustment in Venezuela between 1989 and 1993," mimeograph, World Bank Project on Governance and Successful Adjustment, Caracas, November 1994. For Caldera, Corrales, "Presidents, Ruling Parties, and Party Rules"; and Pedro Palma, "La economía venezolana en el quinquenio 1994–1998: De una crisis a otra," *Nueva economía* 8 (April 1999), pp. 97–158.

a. Interim president Velásquez introduced sweeping economic reforms, but his tenure was too brief (less than six months) for him to implement them all, and his successor reversed many of those that had been introduced.

laws that perpetuate investment barriers. The nonoil private sector is undiversified, noncompetitive, and leery of investing except in conjunction with fiscal support from the state. Poverty and inequality levels, always high, continued to deteriorate steadily in the 1990s. In 1997 real wages were approximately 60 percent lower than in 1978.[13]

Another unresolved problem is a built-in mechanism for procyclical fiscal policies. Fiscal policy tends to be highly procyclical in most of Latin America.[14] But in Venezuela this problem has been especially pronounced due to Venezuela's status as a petrostate.[15] During oil booms, the economy automatically expands (because of PDVSA's higher production levels), and so do fiscal revenues. The increase in fiscal revenues inevitably prompts loose spending, thus adding an unnecessary stimulus to aggregate demand.

When oil prices decline, economic activity contracts (as PDVSA slows down production), as do fiscal revenues, which leads to cutbacks that, in turn, exacerbate the economic slowdown. Moreover, the government's perpetual determination to maintain an overvalued exchange rate gives rise to higher interest rates and hence greater expenses for debt servicing. And so the pattern continues until the situation becomes unsustainable and the government is forced to undertake a massive devaluation.[16]

This pronounced procyclical bias of public finances points to the strong need for a mechanism to generate savings during periods of economic boom. As of 1998, no reform program had ever delivered such a mechanism, another sign of the modesty and shortcomings of all previous reform efforts.

New Hurdles

Some of Venezuela's economic problems in the late 1990s were typical not so much of Latin American nations as of reform-lagging nations. A common problem of nations that repeatedly try but fail to reform is the emergence of an asymmetrical institutional setting. A result of ax-relax-collapse cycles is that some economic institutions and rules became very modernized, while others remained unreformed altogether. This helps explain some discrepancies in policy outcomes. For example, trade liberalization advanced in the manufacturing sectors, but experienced setbacks in agriculture.[17] The country was highly integrated into the international economy but lacked mechanisms for dealing with external volatility. Foreign investment was completely liberalized, but various economic sectors remained plagued with nontransparent regulations that discouraged it. The central bank was highly autonomous, but the ministry of finance remained susceptible to lobbying pressures. In short, reformed and unreformed economic sectors and state institutions uneasily coexisted.

Perhaps the main consequence of the ax-relax-collapse pattern of reform was the erosion of the credibility of the state, politicians, and reform proposals.[18] This was evident both among high-profile economic agents, such as business leaders, and the general public. The former concluded, based on actual experience, that the government was more likely to falter on its reform commitments than to honor them. They thus behaved accordingly, balking at the notion of cooperating with any government announcement. Repeated reform failure also ensured the continuance, and possibly the

Table 6-3. *Confidence in Professional Leaders, Caracas, April 1998*
Percent

Professional	Respondents expressing confidence
University teacher	77
Doctor	75
School teacher	70
Newscaster	68
Journalist	56
Pollster	54
Judge	29
Police officer	21
Union leader	17
Public official	17
Politician	10
Cabinet minister	9

Source: Consultores 21, "Insight 21," *VenEconomy Monthly,* vol. 16 (December 1998), p. 9.

increase, of reform opposition among the general public. The fact that no reform program ever delivered any lasting corrective allowed reform opponents to gain ground, not lose it. Reform opponents were able to argue, groundlessly but convincingly, that Venezuela's ailments were caused by the announced reforms, conveniently avoiding the real diagnosis, which was that the ailments were the result of the failure to carry out the reforms.

This tarnished the credibility of reform efforts. Common citizens came to equate *adjustment*, a word that they had been hearing for the past twenty years, with too much *sacrifice* for nothing in return, just one more scam whereby corrupt politicians pass on the cost of adjustment to the citizenry, only to squander the proceeds. Table 6-3 shows the dramatically low levels of public confidence in cabinet ministers and politicians. Given that ministers and politicians are the "authors" of reforms, these low levels of confidence reveal the size of the state's credibility gap by 1998. All of this was the result of twenty years of repeated ax-relax-collapse cycles.

Venezuela's Latest Round of Reforms: Agenda Venezuela

Venezuela's most recent round of market-oriented reforms, Agenda Venezuela (1996–98), fell into the same ax-relax-collapse cycle. Like previous reform attempts, it initially made impressive headway. For instance, it brought Venezuela out of one of its most sinister economic periods (1994–96), when the state mismanaged a banking crisis by applying inconsistent, nontransparent bailouts. In the end, the total bill of the bailout was 15 percent of gross national product, one of the costliest state bailouts ever to occur.[19] Agenda Venezuela also opened the oil sector to foreign direct investment (the so-called *apertura petrolera*). International investors responded by bringing capital back into the country.

However, Agenda Venezuela soon fell into the customary relax mode. Few additional macro- and microeconomic reforms were implemented in 1997. Privatization, deregulation, tax reforms, fiscal reform, and civil service reforms were timid. Wages in the public sector were not kept in check. A legislative proposal to create the Fondo de Estabilización Macroeconómica, which would have counteracted the procyclical nature of economic management and helped save some of the $6–$8 billion in oil windfalls received in 1997, sat idle in Congress for most of 1997.

In addition, Agenda Venezuela, like previous reform attempts, generated new problems. Prominent among these was oil's continued domination, to the detriment of the nonoil sectors. As part of the *apertura petrolera*, the government agreed to finance a ten-year expansion of PDVSA that would double oil production capacity to 6.4 million barrels per day, a total investment of $65 billion. The administration repeated the mistake of the 1970s of abusing oil-subsidized investments to cover up fiscal disarray. The progress made since 1990 in diversifying the economy suffered a setback: after falling from 19 percent in 1990 to almost 7 percent in 1995, the share of oil revenues in public accounts bounced back to 14 percent by 1997. Furthermore, the massive state presence in the oil sector crowded out private investment, as evidenced by the contraction of private investment during 1993–97.

Political Bottlenecks of Agenda Venezuela

Why did Agenda Venezuela repeat the relax-collapse phases of previous reform efforts? Some analysts blame the oil boom of 1997 for presumably having reduced the urgency of reformers to continue their mission.[20] Some blame the personal hesitancy—or embarrassment—of President Caldera, who came to office in 1994 strongly denouncing the market reforms of the early 1990s and spent his first two years in office dismantling them. Caldera then switched to market reforms in 1996—after ruining the economy with statist policies. But many argue that he was neither a true convert nor humble enough to accept that he was wrong—hence his hesitance about implementing market reforms in 1997. However, most policymakers deny that either the oil boom or the president had any such impact. The reform czar Teodoro Petkoff actually saw the oil boom as a welcome cushion—an opportunity to move ahead, rather than relax the reforms.[21] Moreover, reformers also argue that while Caldera was never enormously enthusiastic, he never presented any obstacles to the reform plans proposed by cabinet members. Thus neither oil nor presidential hesitancy adequately explains the failure of Agenda Venezuela.

The most important reason that Agenda Venezuela entered a relax phase was the same as in previous reform cycles: ailments in the relationship between the state and political parties. In the early 1980s Venezuela's strong party system began to decay.[22] The problem was not that dominant parties were disappearing, but rather that they were becoming increasingly closed off to new leadership and initiatives. Consequently, their level of support declined steadily, as measured by levels of party loyalty, electoral abstention rates, distrust of politicians, and public opinion support for the coup attempt of February 1992.[23] Internal party rules, which exempted party leaders from having to compete electorally in order to earn leadership positions, precluded the rotation of party leaders. Party leadership thus remained virtually unchanged, even when parties were suffering setbacks at the polls. This distinguished Venezuela's major parties from the leading party in Mexico, the Partido Revolucionario Institucional (PRI), which, although less democratic historically, always underwent rotation of leaders with every new administration.[24]

This disjuncture between an increasingly disillusioned electorate and rigidities within the parties that precluded rotation of leadership and ideas was at the root of Venezuela's reform travails. Under conditions of societal discontent and persistent economic crisis, less rigid political parties would have undergone some form of internal transformation. But in Venezuela, old party leaders remained entrenched, essentially guaranteeing the continuity of outdated ideas. These entrenched leaders reacted to declines in societal support not by adapting their thinking, but by resorting to old-fashioned formulas, namely, stepping up populist appeals. They operated on the mistaken assumption that votes could be regained through traditional, corporatist-based handouts rather than by demonstrating competence in solving public policy crises. It was hard for individuals interested in pursuing a different strategy to obtain positions of leadership in the dominant parties.

By 1993, anti-party sentiment peaked. Caldera capitalized on this sentiment by cobbling together an alliance between a small leftist party (Movimiento al Socialismo, or MAS) and a last-minute coalition of independent leftist-nationalist parties and forces (Convergencia). The move was a successful electoral strategy but a terrible recipe for governability. This electoral formula gave Caldera a weak and fragmented political grounding once in office (Convergencia–MAS came in third place in Congress, and MAS began to split after the announcement of Agenda Venezuela).

Thus two major political party ills converged under the Caldera administration: the tendency of both ruling and opposition parties to cling to old leaders and hence old formulas; and the tendency of the ruling party to fracture over economic policy. This latter problem overwhelmed the Pérez administration, as sectors of his own ruling party, Acción Democrática (AD), repudiated his reforms and hence his government.[25] But Caldera, too, became a victim of a similar dislocation in executive-ruling party relations: by 1998, Convergencia essentially disintegrated, and MAS defected to the ranks of Hugo Chávez.

With these difficulties at the party level, even the most capable and reform-minded "technopol" would have had a hard time implementing reforms. Sound reform proposals encountered virulent opposition from the ruling coalition and opposition parties alike. Caldera tried to seek the support of the very same traditional parties that he had campaigned against— AD and the Social Christian party, COPEI—but they sold their support at a very high price. They typically approved reforms only when they were granted important concessions—and that ultimately derailed the reforms. For example, opposition parties agreed to the *apertura petrolera* only in return for a 116 percent increase in salary for oil workers—many of whom were members of AD-dominated unions. This concession flew in the face of inflationary targets that had been set by the central bank.[26] By August 1998, when the shocks hit, more than fifty key reform bills sat idle in Congress, including the crucial Fondo de Estabilización Macroeconómica.[27]

Ailments at the level of political parties—namely, the stranglehold of old party elites despite significant socioeconomic changes—thus explain Venezuela's repeated ax-relax-collapse cycle as well as its susceptibility to the 1998 shocks. Venezuela started 1998 with a pending agenda of structural reforms, including some basic first-generation market reforms (fiscal streamlining and deregulation, for example), as well as a set of Venezuela-specific reforms (for example, Fondo de Estabilización Macroeconómica). Furthermore, Agenda Venezuela generated its own set of problems, specifically, greater reliance on oil, which unnecessarily magnified the impact of the 1998 oil price drop. The credibility problem of the state and politicians reached yet another peak. Understandably, economic agents lost all trust in the government's capacity to deliver. Popular sectors, for their part, were simply fed up with reform efforts that never worked. Hence the most antireform, antiparty presidential candidate of 1998, Hugo Chávez, rose to the top in the polls, in turn infusing new levels of uncertainty at home and abroad. All of this was the direct consequence of the ax-relax-collapse cycle of reform efforts.

The State's Response: The Central Bank to the Rescue

Once the shocks hit, Venezuela faced two policy options: announce a package based on devaluation plus deeper structural reforms (the IMF solution), or simply defend the bolivar. At the heart of the matter was the need to decide between moving toward a more flexible exchange rate regime—following in the footsteps of Mexican and Brazilian policymakers—or upholding the existing quasi-fixed exchange rate regime.

Since the 1980s Venezuela has experimented with all kinds of exchange rate regimes: multiple, controlled exchange rates (1983–88); free but stable exchange rates (1989–92); crawling peg rates (1992–94); and fixed, controlled exchange rates (1994–96).[28] That Caldera would set exchange rate controls in 1994–96 was surprising, given Venezuela's dismal experience with such controls in the 1980s.[29] Indeed, exchange rate controls during 1994–96 reproduced some of the same distortions that had arisen from exchange rate controls in the 1980s: negative real interest rates, black currency markets, declining reserves, the accumulation of liabilities by the central bank, capital flight, and increasing inflation (which reached almost 150 percent at the start of 1996).[30]

Shortly after Agenda Venezuela was launched, officials allowed the exchange rate to float for a few months to signal a return to economic freedom. After testing the real value of the bolivar, the central bank anchored the exchange rate in mid-1996, thereby switching to a "tightly managed" exchange rate system based on bands and a preannounced depreciation rate (*paridad central*). The depreciation rate was moved according to a set percentage each month that was well below inflation rates. The exchange rate thus became a tool to combat inflation or, more specifically, to offset fiscal profligacy.[31] Because the government proved unable to keep fiscal spending in check, the central bank took it upon itself to absorb inflationary pressures by keeping the price of dollars low. The bands were set at plus or minus 7.5 percent of international parity, and promises were made that the exchange rate would never be allowed to cross these bands.

Although technically a free exchange rate regime, in reality the system was a quasi-fixed one. Because the Venezuelan state (through the central bank) holds a quasi monopoly in the supply of foreign exchange (accounting for 85 percent of exports), it has enormous leverage in determining the actual exchange rate.[32] Throughout 1997 the central bank used this leverage to ensure that the exchange rate remained relatively flat. In fact, the bank lowered the central parity three times (in January, July, and December) and even lowered the rate of depreciation for 1997. One result was that annual inflation declined from 112.3 percent in 1996 to 17.3 percent at the end of 1997. This created a sense of triumphalism among the central bank staff.

The shocks of 1998 put an end to this optimistic mood. The demand for dollars skyrocketed, pushing the exchange rate from 504 bolivars to one U.S. dollar in December 1997 to 582 bolivars to the dollar at the end of August 1998, far outpacing the targeted depreciation rate set by the bank (see figure 6-5). The government faced the crucial policy question of whether to devalue or to sell enough dollars to prevent a devaluation. In economic theory, exchange rate flexibility is regarded as a more appropriate policy for dealing with external monetary shocks, whereas a fixed exchange rate is deemed more appropriate for domestic monetary shocks.[33] The problem was that Venezuela was experiencing both shocks simultaneously. Theory, therefore, offered little help.

The IMF recommended devaluation plus reforms, hopeful that this option would address both the economic and the political sources of the crisis.[34] Many economists and influential actors (PDVSA, speculators, exporters, presidential candidates, policy analysts) supported the IMF recommendation. These actors reiterated in public forums that the currency was overvalued, lending credence to the need for a devauation. However, the government rejected this option, choosing instead to defend the bolivar.

Figure 6-5. *The Band System for Venezuela's Exchange Rate, July 1996–September 1999*

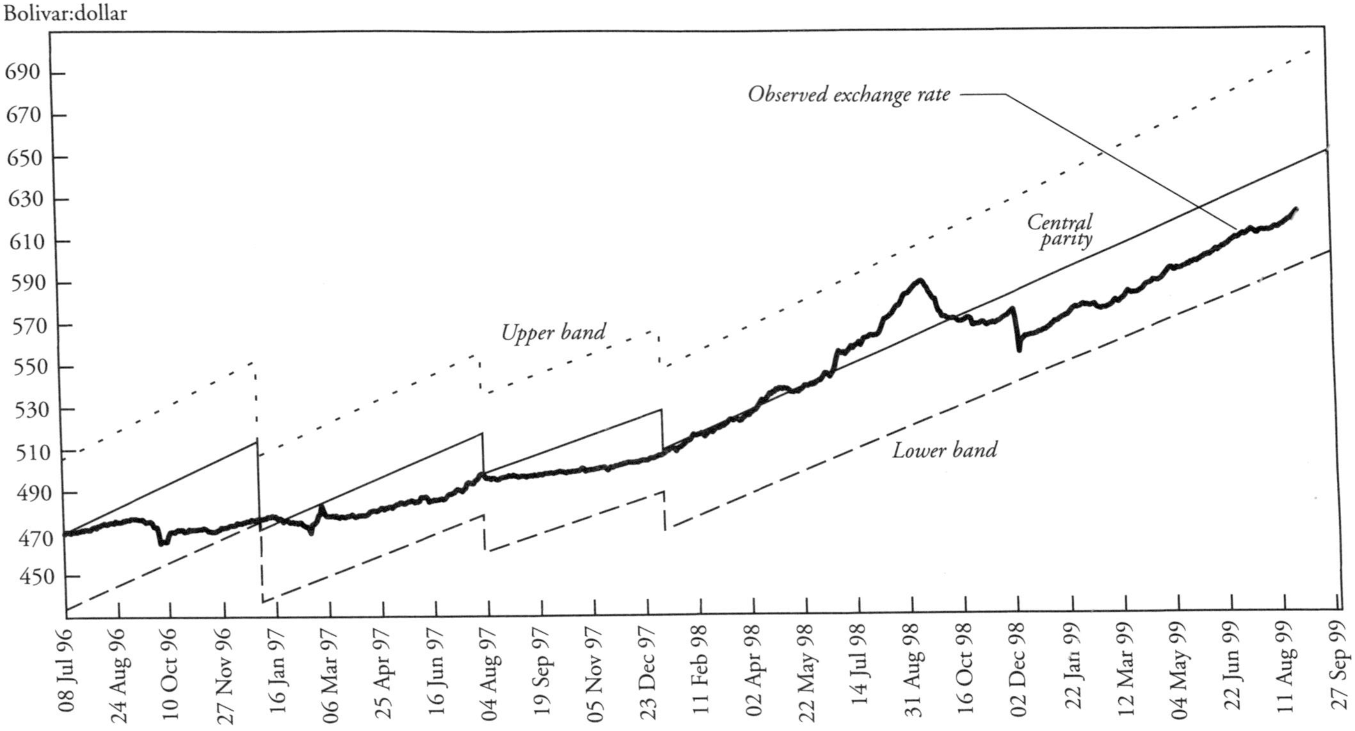

Bolivar:dollar

Source: Metroeconómica, Caracas.

Why? The answer has to do with three sets of considerations: (1) the expected costs and benefits of each policy; (2) the quest for credibility; and (3) the odds of failure of each policy (see table 6-4).

Expected Costs and Benefits

Political economists commonly argue that governments will avoid policies that generate concentrated costs—that is, policies whose costs fall directly and intensely on a concentrated group of actors.[35] Avoiding a devaluation somewhat contradicts this argument. If successful, defending a currency against a speculative attack imposes concentrated losses on domestic financial speculators, who lose enormous sums once they realize that their new assets (dollars) will not increase in value. In the politics of exchange rate choice, therefore, governments consider more than just cost concentration issues. They also consider the expected benefits.

Venezuelan officials estimated that the economic benefits of a devaluation were minimal. In the past, a devaluation of the bolivar would have had an immediate positive impact on the fiscal deficit: it would have allowed PDVSA to obtain more bolivars for its dollars, which increased PDVSA's tax contributions because those contributions are based on earnings converted to bolivars. This benefit was no longer plausible after 1996 because service on the foreign debt was high enough to offset any gains from PDVSA contributions.

In contrast, the economic and political costs of devaluation plus reforms were deemed excessive. Economically, the government estimated that a devaluation would unleash a sudden "inflationary shock" by way of higher import prices, and this was deemed unacceptable.[36] One of the consequences of Venezuela's trade liberalization in 1989 was that imports became a predominant component of household consumption. By automatically increasing the price of imports, a devaluation would deliver an immediate blow to the purchasing power of common citizens.

The government understood the costs of defending the currency—deepening the recession and eroding further the competitiveness of the nonoil sector. But policymakers reasoned that these ailments already existed early in 1998, and hence the defense of the bolivar "would not add to the list of problems of Venezuela."[37] Moreover, given that the administration was on its way out of office and had no presidential candidate for the upcoming elections, it thus had few incentives to be altruistic toward the next administration. And, whereas the main losers of a devaluation

Table 6-4. To Devalue or Not to Devalue, 1998

Action	Benefits	Costs	Odds of worst-case scenario
No devaluation	Contains the crisis; signals credibility; keeps inflation under control	Speculators penalized; nonoil exporters lose competitiveness; economic recession deepens (two latter costs could be passed on to the next administration)	*Medium to low:* central bank has institutional endowments to withstand the crisis—reserves, quasi monopoly, legal and actual independence, track record of policy consistency
Devaluation	Minimal impact on public finances; reduces overvaluation; supports exporters; speculators profit	Higher inflation, especially in consumption goods, affecting low-income groups; deterioration of other macroeconomic variables; credibility deficit grows	*High:* given high political uncertainty and poor fiscal credibility, devaluation automatically fuels suspicions that government lacks control

would be low-income groups who would have to confront immediate price hikes, the main losers under a scenario of policy continuity were speculators who had bet against the bolivar and who would not be decisive in the elections. The government had little interest in scoring popularity points with speculators.

Credibility Gains

Perhaps more important than questions of costs and benefits were issues of credibility. New thinking in political economy suggests that governments strive to signal credibility as a way of obtaining sectoral cooperation for public policies. That is, governments seek to convince economic agents that they will not use discretion in policymaking to violate promises for short-term advantages.[38] Given that the reform effort had entered another "relax" phase in 1997, the government estimated correctly that its credibility deficit was acute. The government was keen to reduce, or at least contain, this credibility deficit. A devaluation, in essence a break in the exchange rate regime, would have eroded credibility further. The exchange rate regime had been the one exemplar of policy continuity since mid-1996, the one promise that the government had kept. Having broken so many other promises, the government could not afford one more round of default.

Lawrence Broz has recently argued that in contexts of "opaque public decision-making" (that is, where actors cannot easily discern and exact punishment for instances in which rules are being broken), governments often opt for a fixed exchange rate as a mechanism for signaling credibility.[39] This is not because fixed exchange rates are economically efficient— they are not—but because they are highly transparent: actors can easily discern whether the commitment is kept or broken. Fixed exchange rates thus allow governments to buy or borrow credibility in moments of doubt. The greater the opaqueness of public decisionmaking, the greater the need to rely on a fixed exchange rate.

This argument explains Venezuela's decision to stick to a semifixed exchange rate in 1998. At first the argument does not seem to apply, since Broz explicitly relates opaqueness with high levels of undemocratic behavior, which does not fit with Venezuela's status as a democratic regime. However, the case could be made that opaqueness is also related to reform-lagging status. The economic and political problems that arose as a result of Venezuela's repeated reform failures blurred the contours of economic policy, causing effects similar to those of nontransparent political institutions.

Probability of Failure and Accumulated Resolve

Finally, the most decisive factor in explaining the government's decision to avoid a devaluation was its own estimate of the odds of failure for each policy option. The worst-case scenario for both policy options was the same: an inability to contain devaluation expectations, triggering a greater than anticipated devaluation, or "overshooting," of the exchange rate, as occurred in Mexico in 1994. Government officials estimated that this outcome was more likely to occur if a package of devaluation plus reforms was attempted, instead of a policy of defending the exchange rate.

The government realized that it was politically unable to deliver a package of fiscal reforms, certainly not so late in the administration and just before an election. In addition, policymakers were wary of the incompetence and frailty of most other state agencies. The ministry of planning (Cordiplan) could have announced a program of structural reforms, as the IMF suggested, but such a program would have had little credibility given the disarray of public finances, the skepticism of economic agents, and the stranglehold that pressure groups and populist politicians held on fiscal policy.[40] Moreover, implementation would be delayed until the next government took office. So, a devaluation would simply exacerbate the reasons that agents were panicking, thus increasing the chance of a policy failure.

The probability of failure in defending the currency was deemed to be lower. Part of the reason for this estimate had to do with "resource factors" such as the bank's high level of reserves and quasi monopoly over the supply of foreign exchange. However, in the past similar resources had failed to prevent currency crises from turning into maxidevaluations. The reason was that high levels of reserves are easily depletable, as numerous currency crises in the 1990s have proved. In Mexico (1994), Thailand (1997), Russia (1998), and Brazil (1999), the more reserves were employed to stop a speculative attack, the less ammunition remained, and hence the less capacity each state had to signal fortitude. In fact, as reserves decline, speculators have all the more reason to expect a forthcoming devaluation. This is why the use of reserves to stop a currency attack easily exacerbates, rather than counteracts, the expectations for a devaluation.

Resources, then, were not the reason behind the government's higher confidence in a policy of exchange rate defense. Rather than the level of reserves, the government relied on its "accumulated resolve." By this I mean the institutional factors that permitted the central bank to adhere to a chosen policy path. These factors were (1) prior institutional reforms; (2) government-bank coordination; and (3) a track record of policy consistency.

INSTITUTIONAL REFORMS: THE RISE OF LEGAL CENTRAL BANK INDEPENDENCE. The central bank of Venezuela was an example of the asymmetrical institutional setting typical of reform-lagging states: it was one of the few public institutions that had been modernized following a process of reform, yet it operated in the midst of unreformed institutions. In late 1992, during the last months of the Pérez administration, the new "Law of the Central Bank" was approved, establishing the autonomy of the central bank. Previously the central bank had been a highly politicized body: the ministry of finance (the entity primarily in charge of disbursing public funds, and hence the most susceptible to lobbying pressures) had control over the appointment of directors. Moreover, the bank's board of directors included representatives from the business, banking, and labor sectors. All of this essentially guaranteed sectoral and partisan influence over central bank policymaking.

The 1992 reform changed this. Sectoral representatives were removed from the board of directors, and the minister of finance lost control over the appointment of directors. The central bank was entrusted with the mission to "create and maintain monetary, credit and exchange conditions that encourage the stability of the currency."[41] In addition, the bank was banned from engaging in "economic development" roles, such as supplying quasi-fiscal subsidies, offering different services to the private as well as to the public sector, and bailing out insolvent entities. In other words, the 1992 law produced the rise of legal autonomy, which proved to be an asset during the 1998 crisis. Legal autonomy allowed the Bank to eschew the enormous sectoral and partisan clamor for a devaluation.

GOVERNMENT-BANK COORDINATION: THE RISE OF ACTUAL CENTRAL BANK INDEPENDENCE. Legal autonomy is not sufficient to guarantee central bank independence. Governments easily find informal mechanisms to violate central bank autonomy. Thus specialists distinguish between *legal* and *actual* central bank independence. Many argue that the latter depends on other, less structured factors, such as the informal arrangements between the central bank and other parts of government.[42] Indeed, during the first two years of the Caldera administration, the government violated actual central bank independence. For instance, Caldera ignored the central bank's recommendations on how to handle the banking crisis of 1994, forcing the then-president of the bank, Ruth de Krivoy, to resign that May. Caldera also established exchange rate controls against the wishes of the bank, which refused to endorse this policy, compelling the government to hand over to PDVSA the management of the control mechanisms. During 1994–96, the government and the central bank held separate and uncoordinated policy positions. The former was pursuing fiscal expansion and closed-economy policies; the latter was being excluded from key economic policy decisions and forced to take "additional steps to prevent certain variables . . . from veering off the path set by the new Central Bank Law"—the involuntary accumulation of liabilities.[43]

This uncoordinated relationship changed in mid-1996 with Agenda Venezuela. The government and the bank began to work together to design and defend the new currency band. Policy objectives continued to diverge—the government remained unable to contain fiscal profligacy—but government-bank interactions were significantly improved. For the first time, the central bank was allowed to pursue its own policies as it saw fit, with complete support from the national executive. During 1998, Teodoro Petkoff, minister of Cordiplan, repeatedly defended in public every policy pursued by the central bank and condemned its critics. This shift in government–central bank relations from noncoordination to coordination constituted the rise of what Sylvia Maxfield identifies as the two crucial freedoms that central banks require: "independence *from*" and "freedom *to*."[44]

POLICY CONSISTENCY. Once actual independence was established in 1996, the central bank was able to uphold policy consistency—that is, to pursue policies consistent with its intended objectives. The bank's stated objective was to stabilize the currency, absorb excess liquidity, and control inflation. To meet these objectives, governments must uphold a consistent policy mix: willingness to meet the demand for dollars matched by willingness to restrict the supply of credit (by raising interest rates). This policy is politically unpopular because it hinders economic growth. Mexico in 1994 failed to uphold this policy mix, which explains its exchange rate troubles at the end of that year. Although committed to similar objectives, the Mexican government pursued only one component of this package: it met the demand for dollars but not the need to restrict credit. In their effort to avoid a recession, officials in Mexico actually lowered interest rates throughout 1994. Expanding the supply of credit in the context of capital flight and reserve depletion was economically self-defeating. It was also politically unwise, because it signaled a lack of policy resolve. This policy inconsistency helped cause the peso crisis. Venezuela after 1996, on the other hand, adhered to the right policy mix. Interest rates were increased during each currency run of 1998. This was economically costly because it exacerbated the recession, but it was politically fruitful because it allowed the bank to signal resolve.

In short, institutional endowments—legal autonomy, improvement in government-bank coordination, and policy consistency—granted the bank a high degree of accumulated resolve. This is what made government officials confident in the capacity of the central bank to defeat devaluation expectations in the midst of exogenous shocks.[45] And it was this resolve, rather than reserves, that allowed the state to defeat the attack on the currency. Unlike reserves, resolve is a cumulative, not a depletable, resource: the more it is deployed, the more it continues to persuade.

The Demise of Venezuela's Party System and the Future of Economic Reforms

Although Venezuelan authorities succeeded in defending the bolivar, they failed in their most important political objective: preventing the electoral victory of the presidential candidate most hostile to market reform, Hugo Chávez Frías. Chávez comfortably won the presidential election of December 1998 and overwhelmed the opposition in the election for delegates to a new constitutional assembly in July 1999. In the process, Venezuela's "historical parties," AD and COPEI, were decimated. Although these parties made a relatively strong showing in congressional and gubernatorial elections of November 1998, their candidates attracted few votes in the December 1998 presidential race and the July 1999 constitutional assembly elections. Venezuela's new constitution, approved at the end of December 1999, extends the presidential term of office to six years.

Several questions now come to mind. Will Chávez inflict further economic damage by pursuing statist policies? Will he succumb to the same ax-relax-collapse reform pattern that plagued his predecessors? Or will he surprise his detractors and succeed in breaking this cycle for good? Finally, given his expressed affinity for Peruvian president Alberto Fujimori's autocratic, anti-party style, will Chávez pursue reform in a similar authoritarian vein?

If Chávez converts to market economics, just as most of Latin America's presidents in the 1990s did once in office, he will enjoy some favorable political conditions. First, Chávez's supporters are numerous and highly mobilized, and their support for him seems to be more devotional than contractual, based on his personal charisma rather than the expectation of favorable policy results. This grants the president a significant degree of freedom in public policy, including the freedom to break his populist promises. Second, with the virtual collapse of the traditional opposition parties, Chávez has unprecedented room to maneuver. Finally, Chávez enjoys an enviable financial cushion.[46] Whereas President Pérez in 1989 had to address Venezuela's economic problems with a mere $3 billion in reserves, and President Caldera faced a gigantic banking crisis with less than $10 billion in reserves in 1994, Chávez came to office with more than $14 billion in reserves. Moreover, the price of oil skyrocketed to $30 a barrel in mid-2000, a threefold increase since the end of 1998.[47]

One would think that this is an ideal context for reform implementation. Few reform-minded presidents enjoy this unusual combination of high levels of popular support, devastated opposition parties, and a substantial financial cushion. Any market-oriented economist would be tempted to sign on as a member of Chávez's team. Yet three countervailing trends complicate this rosy scenario.

PRESIDENTIAL COMMITMENT. How likely is Chávez to abandon statism? So far, the signs are mixed. On the one hand, as of this writing, Chávez has yet to reverse the economic reform process. He has even defended the central bank's policy. This is a far better record than that of Caldera, who during his first six months in office implemented the most antiliberal economic policies in Latin America in the 1990s. Perhaps the weakening of the organized opposition has softened Chávez's autocratic tendencies, as there is no major organized dissidence to combat. However, Chávez has not unequivocally renounced statist-autocratic tactics.[48] He has upheld *apertura petrolera*, but he has reinstated "buy Venezuelan" laws in the oil sector, reminiscent of the high period of import-substitution industrialization in Latin America.[49] His new constitution grants the state enormous prerogatives in economic affairs. Chávez speaks about the economy in vague terms: "Instead of the market dogma, I propose the development of children and education."[50] He has undermined the autonomy of PDVSA by placing close political allies, including military-related personnel, in the company's management and forcing the resignation of more autonomous directors. And in politics, he has a penchant for issuing bully-like threats against dissidents. Because he fails to make distinctions between "himself," "his administration," and "the people," he seems to imply that criticisms of the first two are equivalent to attacks against the last. During the July 2000 presidential campaign his favorite slogan was, "Tremble, oligarchs."[51]

THE FRAGILITY OF THE RULING COALITION. Like the ruling coalition under Caldera, Chávez's ruling coalition, Polo Patriótico, is an ad hoc, last-minute mélange of small, marginal parties of the left and sectors of the military, with support from defecting factions of some traditional parties. This coalition is therefore likely to confront a similar if not worse structural instability. Two fault lines imperil this coalition and hence any forthcoming reform effort: (1) a civil-military divide; and (2) a reformers versus nonreformers divide. The former already produced the first major political earthquake: in early 2000, a leading member of the "military" wing of the Polo Patriótico, Francisco Arias Cárdenas, broke with the government and launched his bid for the presidency in protest against the "slow pace" of the promised revolution and the excessive influence of civilian leaders. In July 2000, two serving officers of the armed forces openly asked for Chávez's resignation. The latter fault line has not produced major shakedowns yet, but this might change once the government announces a serious economic reform program. None of the parties in the Polo Patriótico is strong, which might compel the Polo's leaders to prefer using state resources to build political machines rather than to pursue reforms. And these parties, like the displaced traditional parties, have been immune to leadership rotation, and thus cannot be counted on to be up to date on current economic thinking. Moreover, what united the alliance was a common desire to destroy AD. Now that much of this is done, it is unclear what else holds them together.

DISCOUNTING THE OPPOSITION. The government might make the mistake of exaggerating the extent to which the opposition has been weakened or destroyed. Although the old parties are weaker, Chávez has not seduced the entire nation. He obtained almost 95 percent of the seats in the elections for the constitutional assembly, but the actual vote count was far less overwhelming: Chávez's candidates obtained 63 percent of the votes in Caracas and 56 percent of the votes in the provinces. In addition, the government failed to prevent a spectacular abstention rate of 54 percent. It was the electoral system and the fragmentation of the opposition, rather than a presumed "overwhelming support of the government," that translated this vote count into 95-percent control of the constitutional assembly.[52] Twenty-nine percent of voters rejected the new constitution.

No member of the opposition supported it, a reflection of the high degree of government-opposition divide in Venezuela.

If Chávez continues to dismiss this dissent, he could very well jeopardize his chances of ever becoming a successful economic reformer. Economic reforms are more lasting not when they are implemented in disregard of the opposition, but when incumbents devise political incentives that persuade opposition forces to cooperate.[53] Bullying the opposition is no way to achieve this.

In short, many handicaps that impeded reform consolidation in the past still persist: wavering presidential commitment, a weak ruling coalition prone to fragmentation, parties with unchanged leadership, and a general disdain toward parties and critics. The path to reform consolidation remains riddled with obstacles.

Conclusion

This chapter has sought to illustrate the perils of being a reform laggard. Venezuela in 1998 was neither a case of lack of reform implementation nor one of reform avoidance but rather one of repeated reform failures, stuck since 1979 in an ax-relax-collapse pattern of reform. This pattern of reforms, attributable to the behavior of political parties, has had ruinous consequences. It has left Venezuela with a core set of unresolved economic problems, an odd coexistence of modernized and traditional sectors and institutions, and an acute crisis of credibility, leading to cynicism toward the state and politicians. This explains why the exogenous shocks of 1997–98 had such a calamitous economic and political effect. Venezuela could not have controlled the Asian crisis, the decline in oil prices, and the timing of the 1998 presidential elections, but its ax-relax-collapse pattern of reform made it particularly susceptible to these shocks and ill equipped to respond.

Standard economic theory dictated a package of devaluation plus structural adjustment as the proper response to these shocks. But the credibility deficit precluded the implementation of this option. Citizens would not believe in it. Parties would not allow it. A devaluation-based adjustment was thus likely to fail.

One benefit of being a repeatedly failed reformer, as opposed to a complete reform avoider, was the gradual emergence of some modernized institutions—themselves legacies of previous reforms—that the government could tap on its behalf. One such institution was a more autonomous central bank. This gave the state its most important asset: the capacity to pursue a restrictive monetary policy and tight exchange rate regime. As a defensive response to external shocks in economic hard times, these policies were less than optimal. But pursuing them made sense given the particular political context. Since 1996 the central bank had demonstrated far more resolve than any other state entity. It was understandable, therefore, that the government would resort to the one state entity that had shown such competence.

In the end, the decision to defend the currency was essentially a political decision to surrender policymaking to the central bank in the face of governmental incompetence in other areas of economic management. The motivations for this choice were similar to those that prompted Argentina to establish the Convertibility Law in 1991: the need to regain the trust of economic agents in a context of limited alternatives and huge credibility gaps.[54] However, the dynamics were different. In Argentina the Convertibility Law was enacted as a mechanism for gaining credibility by tying the hands of policymakers (the law prevents the executive from adjusting the exchange rate regime or using reserves to support it), whereas in Venezuela the logic was to gain credibility through institutional delegation. Because the government could not competently manage the crisis, it yielded to the only authority that had a chance of doing so. This is why the central bank, with its bias for exchange rate defense, emerged as the main protagonist in this story.

Credibility deficits and policy opaqueness help explain Venezuela's decision to cling to defending the currency, but they cannot explain its success in doing so. Argentina, until 1991, Mexico in 1994, Venezuela in 1995–96, Colombia and Ecuador in 1997–98, and Brazil in 1999 are notorious examples of failed efforts. What explains the Venezuelan success in 1998? The answer has to do with the nature of central bank–government relations, specifically, the emergence of legal independence in 1992, actual independence in 1996, and policy consistency in 1998. These institutional endowments allowed the central bank to exhibit resolve, which, more than anything else, allowed it to defeat devaluation expectations at a time when all economic indicators pointed toward the inevitability of a devaluation.

Notwithstanding the central bank's success, Venezuela's economy and political system remain fragile, to say the least. Despite the greater tranquility in international financial markets, the recovery of oil prices, and the end of the electoral period, Venezuela's economic recession actually deepened in 1999. Uncertainty about the economic course of the new administration has translated into a de facto investment strike. According to a poll of industrialists, 23 percent of Venezuelan firms reduced or canceled their investment plans in 1999.[55] The continuing attempt to maintain a restrictive monetary policy and tight exchange rate regime in conjunction with fiscal profligacy and macroeconomic uncertainty is a time bomb. Elsewhere, this combination has proved to be unsustainable in the long run: "One party will have to revise its strategy (give in)."[56] In Venezuela in 1998, neither "party" gave in. Instead, it was the real economy and the political system that gave in, as measured by the depth of the recession, the paralysis of the private sector, the further decline of living standards, and the demise of the party system. Venezuela was able to weather the storm in 1998, and to defend the bolivar, but it is unclear that it is politically better prepared to withstand future shocks.

Notes

1. See W. Max Corden's chapter in this volume.

2. The overall trend in the 1990s has been to move away from fixed exchange rate regimes toward more flexible, market-oriented regimes. Of these, the International Monetary Fund (IMF) distinguishes between very flexible (independent floating exchange rates) and less flexible (managed floating) regimes. Venezuela, together with fifty-three other countries out of one hundred surveyed, belonged to the latter category as of December 1997. International Monetary Fund, *Exchange Rate Arrangements and Currency Convertibility: Developments and Issues* (Washington, 1999), pp. 25–26.

3. For general overviews of Latin America's transition to the market, see William P. Glade, "The Latin American Economies Restructure, Again," in Jan Knippers Black, ed., *Latin America: Its Problems and Its Promise* (Boulder: Westview Press, 1998), pp. 145–61; Inter-American Development Bank, *Latin America after a Decade of Reforms* (Washington, 1996); Sebastian Edwards, *Crisis and Reform in Latin America: From Despair to Hope* (Oxford University Press, 1995); Augusto Varas, "Latin America: Toward a New Reliance on the Market," in Barbara Stallings, ed., *Global Change, Regional Response* (Cambridge University Press, 1995), pp. 272–308; Samuel Morley, Roberto Machado, and Stefano Pettinato, *Indexes of Structural Reform in Latin America,* Serie Reformas Económicas, vol. 12 (Santiago: Economic Commission for Latin America and the Caribbean, 1999); Philip Oxhorn and Graciela Ducatenzeiler, "The Problematic Relationship between Economic and Political Liberalization: Some Theoretical Considerations," in Philip Oxhorn and Pamela K. Starr, eds., *Markets and Democracy in Latin America: Conflict or Convergence?* (Boulder: Lynne Rienner, 1999); and William Ratliff, "Development and Civil Society in Latin America and Asia," *Annals of the American Academy of Political and Social Science,* vol. 565 (September 1999), pp. 91–112.

4. A study of eleven Latin American countries reveals that Venezuela had one of the most inflexible exchange rate responses to the Russian crisis. Venezuela's exchange rate

changed by 1.51 percent between July and October 1998. Only four countries were more inflexible: Argentina (0.00), Chile (–0.58), Panama (0.00), and Uruguay (1.40). Other countries experienced greater changes: Brazil (2.65), Colombia (12.87), Costa Rica (2.78), Ecuador (25.72), Mexico (13.90), and Peru (4.78). See Michael Gavin, "Latin American Central Banks: Reticent to React," *Latin American Economic Policies,* vol. 7 (Washington: Inter-American Development Bank, 1999), p. 3.

5. Stephan Haggard, *Pathways from the Periphery: The Politics of Growth in Newly Industrializing Countries* (Cornell University Press, 1990), p. 45.

6. International Monetary Fund, *World Economic Outlook: October 1999* (Washington, 1999). Unless otherwise indicated, economic statistics about Venezuela are obtained from various Banco Central de Venezuela sources. All dollar amounts are U.S. dollars.

7. Congreso de la República, *Informe de coyuntura, primer trimestre de 1999,* Series Informes, 99-005 (Caracas, April 1999).

8. *VenEconomy Monthly,* vol. 16 (April 1999), p. 8.

9. See Jennifer McCoy, "Chávez and the End of 'Partyarchy' in Venezuela," *Journal of Democracy,* vol. 10 (July 1999), pp. 64–77.

10. The Caracas stock index dropped from 10,489 points in September 1997 to 4,802 points in June 1998.

11. See Brian F. Crisp and Daniel H. Levine, "Democratizing the Democracy? Crisis and Reform in Venezuela," *Journal of Interamerican Studies and World Affairs,* vol. 40 (Summer 1998), pp. 27–63; Jennifer McCoy and William C. Smith, "From Deconsolidation to Reequilibration? Prospects for Democratic Renewal in Venezuela," in Jennifer McCoy, Andrés Serbin, William C. Smith, and Andrés Stambouli, eds., *Venezuelan Democracy under Stress* (New Brunswick, N.J.: Transaction Books, 1995), pp. 237–83; Richard S. Hillman, *Democracy for the Privileged: Crisis and Transition in Venezuela* (Boulder: Lynne Rienner, 1994); Moisés Naím and Ramón Piñango, *El caso venezolano: Una ilusión de armonía* (Caracas: Ediciones IESA, 1985); and Miriam Kornblith, "Deuda y democracia en Venezuela: Los sucesos del 27 y 28 de febrero de 1989," *Cuadernos del CENDES,* vol. 10 (1989), pp.17–34.

12. Alberto Alesina and Allan Drazen, "Why Are Stabilizations Delayed?" *American Economic Review,* vol. 81 (December 1991), pp. 1170–88.

13. Pedro Palma, "La economía venezolana en el quinquenio 1994–1998: De una crisis a otra," *Nueva Economía,* vol. 8 (April 1999), pp. 97–158.

14. Michael Gavin and Roberto Perotti, "Fiscal Policy in Latin America," in Ben S. Bernanke and Julio Rotemberg, eds., *NBER Macroeconomics Annual 1997* (Cambridge: MIT Press, 1997).

15. Terry Lynn Karl, "The Venezuelan Petro-State and the Crisis of 'Its' Democracy," in McCoy, Serbin, Smith, and Stambouli, eds., *Venezuelan Democracy under Stress,* pp. 33–55.

16. Congreso de la República, *Informe de coyuntura.*

17. Javier Corrales and Imelda Cisneros, "Corporatism, Trade Liberalization, and Sectoral Responses: The Case of Venezuela, 1989–1999," *World Development,* vol. 27 (December 1999), pp. 2099–122.

18. For the impact of credibility deficits on state-society relations during reform processes, see Dani Rodrik, "Promises, Promises: Credible Policy Reform via Signaling," *Economic Journal,* vol. 99 (1989), pp. 756–72.

19. See Gustavo García, with Rafael Rodríguez and Silvia Salvato, *Lecciones de la crisis bancaria de Venezuela* (Caracas: Ediciones IESA, 1998).

20. See Palma, "La economía venezolana." Many political economists are convinced that petrostates in general are inherently handicapped when it comes to introducing reforms that address the volatility associated with oil booms and busts. However, some petrostates manage oil cycles better than others, suggesting that political factors such as characteristics of the state, more so than dependence on oil, determine how nations cope with this "resource curse." For an excellent review of these issues, see Michael L. Ross, "The Political Economy of the Resource Curse," *World Politics,* vol. 51 (January 1999), pp. 297–322.

21. Teodoro Petkoff (minister of planning [Cordiplan] during Agenda Venezuela), interview by author, Caracas, August 1999.

22. See Michael Coppedge, "Prospects for Democratic Governability in Venezuela," *Journal of Interamerican Studies and World Affairs,* vol. 36 (Summer 1994), pp. 39–64; Miriam Kornblith and Daniel H. Levine, "The Life and Times of the Party System," in Scott Mainwaring and Timothy Scully, eds., *Building Democratic Institutions: Parties and Party Systems in Latin America* (Stanford University Press, 1995), pp. 37–71; José E. Molina and Carmen Pérez, "Evolution of the Party System in Venezuela, 1946–1993," *Journal of Interamerican Studies and World Affairs,* vol. 40 (Summer 1998), pp. 1–26; Ángel Eduardo Álvarez, "La crisis de hegemonía de los partidos políticos venezolanos," in Ángel E. Álvarez, ed., *El sistema político venezolano: Crisis y transformaciones* (Caracas: Universidad Central de Venezuela, Instituto de Estudios Políticos, 1996); and Crisp and Levine, "Democratizing the Democracy."

23. Enrique A. Baloyra, "Deepening Democracy with Dominant Parties and Presidentialism: The Venezuelan Regime in a Period of Turbulence," in Kurt von Mettenheim and James Malloy, eds., *Deepening Democracy in Latin America* (University of Pittsburgh Press, 1998), pp. 38–54.

24. Javier Corrales, "El Presidente y su gente: Conflicto y cooperación en los ámbitos técnico y político en Venezuela, 1989–1993," *Nueva sociedad,* vol. 152 (November–December 1997), pp. 93–107.

25. Javier Corrales, "Presidents, Ruling Parties, and Party Rules: A Theory on the Politics of Economic Reform in Latin America," *Comparative Politics,* vol. 32 (January 2000), pp. 127–50.

26. Petkoff, interview.

27. Herbert Koeneke, "Congressional Report Card: A Failure, and Little to Learn From," *VenEconomy Monthly,* vol. 15 (September 1998), pp. 15–16.

28. José Guerra, "Síntesis de la política cambiaria de Venezuela," *Monetaria,* vol. 20 (January–March, 1997), pp. 95–115.

29. See Guerra, "Síntesis"; and Agustín Beroes, *RECADI: La gran estafa* (Caracas: Planeta, 1990).

30. Banco Central de Venezuela (BCV), *1998 Year-End Address, President of the Central Bank of Venezuela* (Caracas: 1998); and Herbert Koeneke, "Bad Balance for Caldera Administration," *VenEconomy Monthly,* vol. 16 (January 1999), pp. 3–6.

31. Antonio Casas-González, "Política monetaria y cambiaria en Venezuela," paper presented at the seminar Venezuela Competitiva, Venezuelan Embassy, Santiago, Chile, December 1997.

32. Roberto Bottome, "Foreign Exchange Markets: Not So Free," *VenEconomy Monthly,* vol. 15 (March 1998), pp. 12–13.

33. Beth V. Yarbrough and Robert M. Yarbrough, *The World Economy: Trade and Finance,* 4th ed. (Fort Worth: Dryden Press, 1997).

34. Antonio Casas-González, then president of the central bank, interview by author, Caracas, August 4, 1999.

35. James Q. Wilson, *Political Organizations* (Basic Books, 1973).

36. See interview with Teodoro Petkoff in César Miguel Rondón, *País de estreno: 37 entrevistas antes que el destino del país nos alcance* (Caracas: Los Libros de El Nacional, 1998), p. 255.

37. Petkoff, interview.

38. For a discussion of the importance of signaling a commitment to reform, see Rodrik, "Promises, Promises"; and Mariano Tommasi and Andrés Velasco, "Where Are We in the Political Economy of Reform?" *Journal of Policy Reform,* vol. 1 (1996).

39. Lawrence Broz, "Political Institutions and the Transparency of Monetary Policy Commitments," paper presented at the annual meeting of the American Political Science Association, Atlanta, Ga., September 2–5, 1999.

40. In September 1998, the Congress passed a "special powers law" (*ley habilitante*) authorizing the national executive to enact eight different reforms by decree, including the much-needed Fondo de Estabilización Macroeconómica. However, this congressional commitment to reform was too little, too late, and too ephemeral. It was too little because it did not fully resolve the fiscal deficit, authorizing personnel spending that far exceeded expected increases in tax collections. It was too late because it happened when the crisis was coming to an end. And it was too ephemeral because before the year was over, the same Congress approved seven new credits, which meant that the final 1998 budget produced the same level of spending as projected at the start of the fiscal year (see Congreso de la República, *Informe de coyuntura*).

41. "The Law of the Central Bank of Venezuela," *Official Gazette* (Caracas), December 4, 1992, article 2.

42. Alex Cukierman, Steven B. Webb, and Bilin Neyapti, "Measuring the Independence of Central Banks and Its Effects on Policy Outcomes," *World Bank Economic Review,* vol. 6 (September 1992), pp. 393–401; Alex Cukierman, *Central Bank Strategy, Credibility, and Independence: Theory and Evidence* (MIT Press, 1994).

43. Banco Central de Venezuela, *1998 Year-End Address by the President of the Central Bank of Venezuela* (Caracas, December 18, 1998), p. 4.

44. Sylvia Maxfield, "A Brief History of Central Bank Independence in Developing Countries," in Andreas Schedler, Larry Diamond, and Marc F. Plattner, eds., *The Self-Restraining State* (Boulder: Lynne Rienner, 1999), p. 285.

45. For recent research probing the correlation between central bank independence and economic performance, see Alberto Alesina and Lawrence H. Summers, "Central Bank Independence and Macroeconomic Performance: Some Comparative Evidence," *Journal of Money, Credit, and Banking* (May 1993), pp. 151–62; and Cukierman, *Central Bank Strategy.* Less attention has been devoted to the correlation between central bank independence and exchange rate policy than this chapter suggests might exist.

46. McCoy, "Chávez."

47. The Chávez administration had a lot to do with this dramatic turnaround in the price of oil. Criticizing the Chávez administration for its policy of "inundating the market," Chávez's minister of energy, Alí Rodríguez, lobbied OPEC and non-OPEC members to cut down production. These efforts succeeded, sending oil prices to the highest levels since the Gulf War. See Larry Rohter, "Venezuelan Calls Tune in OPEC's Price Tactics," *New York Times*, April 7, 2000, p. A10.

48. See Javier Corrales, "Hugo Chávez Plays 'Simon Says'," *Hopscotch*, vol. 2, no. 2 (2000).

49. *El nacional*, August 14, 1999.

50. *El universal*, August 10, 1999.

51. *Economist*, July 22–28, 2000, pp. 35–36.

52. The system used for the election of representatives to the constitutional (sometimes referred to as constituent) assembly was "plurinominal." It was not intended to act as a first-past-the-post system. In practice, the candidates with the most votes ended up elected in each district. In addition, no proportional formula was used to ensure representation of nonmajority candidates. The government distributed *chuletas*, Venezuelan slang for crib notes used by students to cheat on exams. These *chuletas* listed the candidates preferred by the government. Pro-government voters voted according to the *chuletas*. Opposition candidates, reluctant to identify themselves with any party label, were not interested in being part of any *chuleta*. As a result, there was no system of coordinating the votes of the opposition, which became dispersed. See Michael Penfold-Becerra, "Constituent Assembly in Venezuela, First Report," mimeograph, Carter Center, Emory University, Atlanta, 1999.

53. Jorge I. Domínguez, "Free Politics and Free Markets in Latin America," *Journal of Democracy*, vol. 9 (Fall 1998), pp. 70–84.

54. Javier Corrales, "Why Argentines Followed Cavallo: A Technopol between Democracy and Economic Reform," in Jorge I. Domínguez, ed., *Technopols: Freeing Politics and Markets in Latin America in the 1990s* (Pennsylvania State University Press, 1997), pp. 49–93.

55. *El nacional*, September 3, 1999.

56. Patricia Pollard, "Central Bank Independence and Economic Performance," *Federal Reserve Bank of St. Louis* (July–August 1993), pp. 21–36.

7

RIORDAN ROETT

The Politics of Exchange Rate Management in the 1990s

THE ESSAYS IN THIS book offer a compelling overview of the exchange rate regimes and policies adopted in four Latin American countries: Mexico, Brazil, Argentina, and Venezuela. W. Max Corden's chapter provides the theoretical framework needed to understand the dilemmas that policymakers confront in setting exchange rate policy as well as a summary of the range of available policy choices: the fixed but adjustable regime, the firmly fixed rate regime, and the floating exchange rate regime. The four country cases analyzed here were chosen because they represent variations on the three main options for exchange rate management, in terms of both policy choice and economic outcome. A fourth policy choice—dollarization—is addressed only in passing in this book, because the debate over dollarization is still incipient in Latin America. Proposals recently put forth by Argentina and Ecuador, for example, have met with little enthusiasm at the U.S. Treasury Department and Federal Reserve Bank.[1] As the experience of the European Union and the literature on optimum currency areas suggest, proposals in favor of a common currency are more credible when the countries in question have long-standing integration ties, or at least much stronger ties than either of these countries now has with the United States.[2]

Beginning his analysis, Corden discusses two main dimensions of exchange rate policy, the nominal anchor approach and the real targets approach, each of which has its advantages and disadvantages. For the nominal anchor approach to work, monetary discipline and labor market credibility are critical. Of particular importance for Latin America, fiscal deficits cannot be financed by money creation. The nominal anchor approach, whereby the exchange rate serves as the anchor for stabilizing the country's inflation rate, will collapse in the absence of fiscal discipline. For all four case studies, this challenge has often been overwhelming.

A variation of the nominal anchor approach is the use of a crawling peg. Employing a peg means that the rate at which the currency is steadily devalued is predetermined at less than the initial rate of inflation; thus the rate of inflation of tradable good prices will slowly decline. The use of the nominal anchor can play a critical role in reducing inflation, but the disadvantage is that the cost of failure is very high—a serious loss of foreign exchange reserves, rising unemployment, and falling output.

For the real targets approach, the nominal exchange rate varies to achieve real targets. But if there is a shock—a decline in the terms of trade, for example—a real depreciation will probably be required to improve the current account. Without a real depreciation, a government must sharply reduce expenditures that could induce a recession and a decline in imports. As Corden points out, the use of the nominal exchange rate as a policy instrument to improve the current account has been at the heart of the balance-of-payments stabilization programs of the International Monetary Fund (IMF).

Corden comments that "Latin American history . . . is littered with the corpses of fixed but adjustable exchange rate regimes." In such regimes, however, the rate is usually not actually fixed; rather, a crawling peg that moves at a predetermined rate of devaluation is employed. But the danger with the crawl is that devaluation is usually needed to offset the real appreciation that occurs or to respond to an adverse shock—a decline in capital flows, perhaps. Generally, the fixed rate is not entirely credible because the possibility of devaluation always exists if the fundamentals are out of balance with market expectations.

As the four case studies demonstrate, governments frequently try to avoid depreciation by raising interest rates, but there are limits on how long this option can be credibly used to hold the rate. At least two of the case studies showed also that confidence in the fixed rate can decline rather quickly. In this event, governments have little choice but to devalue and go to a float. For the government, the political fallout is often as damaging as the harsh economic repercussions.

Another option—used with measured success in Argentina since 1991—is the firmly fixed exchange rate regime. The Argentine currency board is one version of this approach. The great asset of the currency board is its credibility, which normally is backed by a law that ensures that monetary policy is fully determined by the level of foreign exchange reserves. Thus fiscal deficits cannot be monetized and the central bank cannot act as a lender of last resort to the banking system. This regime most closely approximates complete exchange rate stability, and it ensures that the exchange rate is truly a nominal anchor that disciplines monetary policy and checks inflationary expectations.

The major drawback of the firmly fixed exchange rate, from the viewpoint of the country adopting it, is that it precludes the use of the real targets approach. In the face of an adverse shock, the money supply must be allowed to decline (and interest rates to rise), so that domestic demand falls and the current account improves. The risk of a recession is high unless wages and nontradable prices decline.

Finally, a floating rate regime is one that has no exchange rate policy. The nominal anchor approach can be practiced through monetary policy, as Brazil is currently doing. A key challenge for the regime that adopts the float is the volatility involved in response to changing expectations. A variation of the floating regime is the flexible peg regime, whereby the central bank does set a rate but is proactive in its willingness to alter it. Chile has successfully employed this strategy for some time with very reasonable success, as has Colombia.

The four case studies demonstrate that there is little certainty in the world of exchange rate policy. Critical to the credibility of any rate is fiscal discipline, a lesson that Argentina did not learn until early 1991, and Brazil only—and then but partially—in 1994. Venezuela continues to ignore the realities of the need for fiscal adjustment. Mexico has gone from boom to bust to boom and has learned the hard lessons of excessive rigidity in exchange rate policy. Given the stability in Argentina to date, the currency board–fixed exchange rate system may hold appeal—although the trend over the past decade in Latin America has clearly been toward more, not less, flexibility in managing the exchange rate.

As Timothy Kessler writes, it was the Mexican peso devaluation of December 1994 that first drew the attention of emerging-market observers to the new and unexpected volatility of the global capital market. But the Mexican case clearly confirms that the impact of international capital is conditioned by domestic politics and policies. The origins of the crisis began with the decision in 1987 to anchor the peso in an effort to tame inflation. Early in 1989, a crawling peg was introduced. But Mexico's inflation rose well ahead of U.S. inflation, and the impact of the crawl was a gradual but clear appreciation of the peso.

Although there is no dearth of plausible explanations for the decision to defend the peso in the years before the forced devaluation, Kessler is correct in attributing the government's adherence to the exchange rate regime to domestic politics. Devaluations have always been anathema in Mexican politics. Although each of the three preceding presidents had been forced to devalue at the end of their terms, President Carlos Salinas de Gortari and his team were determined not to do so. Large corporations—the backbone of the "success" of the North American Free Trade Agreement (NAFTA)—held high levels of dollar-denominated debt, and Mexico's "social pact" between business, the government, and labor depended on the mainte-nance of the exchange rate anchor. Moreover, the middle classes benefited from the overvalued currency because it helped lower inflation and subsi-dized consumption.

Yet by the end of 1994, the ruling Institutional Revolutionary Party (PRI) had few options but to devalue. Notwithstanding growing trade deficits and volatile capital flows, the imperative of the July 1994 presi-dential race—which the PRI won with the election of Ernesto Zedillo Ponce de León as president—and the inauguration that December ruled against an immediate devaluation. Within three weeks after the new chief executive was sworn in, though, the pressure on the peso was unsustainable and the new and inexperienced economic team took the decision to devalue. Recession, high unemployment, erosion of wages, and a precipi-tate fall in social spending followed. The peso crisis drove the collapse of the nation's banking system, requiring approximately 15 percent of the country's gross domestic product to bail it out.

In the midst of the financial crisis, revelations of banking fraud prolif-erated and the PRI lost its majority in the lower house of Congress. As it turned out, the context of renewed economic crisis paved the way for more competitive party politics in Mexico. In the 2000 presidential race, a for-midable and legitimate challenge to the government emerged with the can-didacy of Vicente Fox of the National Action Party.

The aftermath of the devaluation, and the PRI's search to regain the political upper hand, led to a successful float of the peso, a more aggressive promotion of exports, and a greater focus on implementing policies to pro-mote the country's competitive standing within NAFTA and other international markets. Apart from triggering efforts to recapitalize the banking system and increase transparency in public accounts, the political result of the peso crisis is that the 2000 election, by all accounts, was the most open and fair election in the country's history. Mexico paid a high price for the December 1994 devaluation, but a better-managed economy and a far healthier political system have apparently emerged out of that tumultuous devaluation.

The long road to Brazil's decision to adopt an exchange rate anchor in 1994 is clearly explained in Eliana Cardoso's chapter. In the early 1990s, "inflation became the main mechanism for managing imbalances that politicians could not or would not correct." As Brazil moved away from twenty-one years of military rule, the reduction of chronic inflation became the principal emphasis of economic policy. Various heterodox shock programs were tried and failed; halfhearted orthodox measures were taken and then abandoned. In spite of the deleterious social consequences of inflation, the economy continued to function, which explains in great part why early efforts at structural change failed.

In 1993 the right individual—Fernando Henrique Cardoso—became Brazil's finance minister, and he and his advisers found a viable solution: the Real Plan. Stabilization went through three phases: a fiscal adjustment, monetary reform, and the use of the exchange rate as a nominal anchor. The economic team—and the new president, Cardoso, elected in late 1994 as a result of the Real Plan—understood the need for fiscal reform if the nominal anchor were to hold. But the reform process ran into strong political opposition in the fragmented Brazilian Congress. The operational deficit worsened, as did the primary surplus. The economic leadership resorted to monetary policy as a substitute for fiscal reform, rationalizing that fiscal reform was necessary but impossible; therefore, monetary policy would have to suffice until the political moment was right for legislative action.

The crunch came as the real exchange rate appreciated, hurting the industrial sector and provoking unemployment. Nevertheless, even in the face of growing trade deficits and declining savings, the political leadership found it difficult to resist the continued use of the exchange rate to keep inflation under control. The key for the government was strong capital inflows, which sustained currency overvaluation and helped policymakers avoid the looming realities.

The moment of truth for Brazil arrived with the Russian devaluation and debt default in August 1998. Brazil's foreign currency reserves dropped precipitately as the government struggled to defend the real in the face of another external shock. Even an unprecedented December 1998 IMF package of $41 billion, geared toward heading off a Mexican-style crash, proved insufficient. The combination of fiscal foot-dragging, fickle capital outflows, record-high interest rates, and general political uncertainty forced the government to adopt a new exchange rate regime. After an initial effort to control the devaluation, the currency floated.

The devaluation was not as disastrous as many had predicted. In 1999, investor confidence was quickly restored by astute monetary policy and long overdue fiscal action by the Congress. The Brazilian government has bought the time necessary to forge ahead with those structural changes that are further needed to preclude another speculative attack on the currency. The danger in the case of Brazil is that political leaders, as in 1994 and 1995, will assume that deeper reforms are no longer a priority, and that the return to growth and the lowering of interest rates will be sufficient to sustain the recovery. Cardoso's essay highlights the risks of succumbing to this mistaken interpretation of the realities of the Brazilian economy. There is time to act, but the political will to do so must be constantly rallied to effectively tackle the remaining tasks on the reform agenda.

Politics played a key role in Argentina's decision to adopt a currency board in April 1991. As Carol Wise comments, a period of hyperinflation (1989–91) was the "culmination of nearly forty years of state-led economic mismanagement and political turmoil." With no alternatives in sight in 1991, President Carlos Menem and Economics Minister Domingo Cavallo gambled in launching a currency board that fixed the peso one-to-one with the U.S. dollar. An important part of the gamble was Cavallo's credibility in the financial markets and the decision by the new team to press forward with a deep program of market reforms, including the redesign of the tax system and trade liberalization. As a result of that 1991 decision, Argentina entered its longest (1991–94) and most robust expansion since 1945. The broad reform coalition that was built on that economic success, coupled with the economic and political stability that the currency board represented, helped guarantee Menem's reelection in 1995.

Then, without warning, the Mexican devaluation of December 1994 sent an unnerving "tequila effect" rippling through Latin America. Menem and Cavallo reacted with alacrity. Interest rates were raised, the federal budget was slashed, the banking system was restructured, and taxes were increased. Even after Cavallo parted company with Menem in mid-1996, his successor, Roque Fernández, was able to sustain the fixed exchange rate through Menem's second term in office. Because the political will existed in

Argentina to move forward with further reforms, the Asian devaluations of 1997 and the Russian meltdown in 1998 were absorbed without crisis. It would take a third systemic shock, the Brazilian devaluation in January 1999, to raise questions for the first time in the decade about the continued feasibility of the currency board. As the devaluation of the real pushed the bilateral exchange rate of the peso up by nearly 18 percent in real terms, the adjustment burden in Argentina was sudden and harsh.

But the memories of hyperinflation were strong. Fernando de la Rúa, the winning candidate of the opposition coalition, Alianza Democrática, in the October 1999 presidential election, indicated that there would be no shift in monetary policy, even though President Menem had suggested the possibility of dollarization as a response to the Brazilian devaluation. De la Rúa, the candidate of a new alliance between the center and left, was helped by the feckless campaign of his Peronist opponent who suggested, at one point, that Argentina should consider a debt moratorium. And the growing concern over corruption, a weak judicial system, and unemployment further hastened the demise of the Peronists at the polls. Following his inauguration, de la Rúa introduced much-needed legislation to rein in provincial finances and deregulate domestic labor markets, which may help address the country's most difficult problems, namely, the lack of competitiveness and the deterioration in income and employment. It remains to be seen whether the de la Rúa government will succeed in coordinating these reforms under the constraints of the currency board. As Wise points out, the answer to this question lies in the ability of policymakers to move more quickly in designing incentives that will enhance productivity and thus correct for the appreciation of the exchange rate under a fixed regime. With the economic rebound in Brazil, and in Argentina's traditional export markets, the economic winds are shifting such that the de la Rúa team will have some breathing space in managing these crucial adjustments.

Venezuela stands in sharp contrast to these other countries in the sense that policymakers have avoided the adoption of a market strategy, as Javier Corrales explains. As a consequence, a series of shocks emanating from Asia and Russia in 1998 had dire results—a sharp increase in capital flight accompanied by volatility in world oil prices. These shocks were exacerbated by the dramatic burgeoning of political risk as the December 1998 presidential elections approached. Poll after poll indicated that the two-party system that had ruled Venezuela for decades would be defeated by Hugo Chávez, an ex-military officer and political outsider who had plotted to overthrow civilian rule back in 1992.

Venezuela fell into a deep recession, the culmination of decades of what Corrales calls the "ax-relax-collapse" cycle of reform. At the heart of this pattern is the country's long-standing dependence on oil revenues, to the extent that national wealth continues to stem from natural resources rather than labor productivity or industrial competitiveness. When faced with adverse oil prices in 1998, the government had little choice but to ax public spending. Once the fiscal accounts reached equilibrium, the policy of fiscal austerity was relaxed, but without any penetrating reform of tax and spending structures. Since the fiscal overhaul was mainly cosmetic, it did not instill confidence in domestic or international markets. An all but certain collapse followed, after which the dreary cycle began anew. This repetitious pattern left successive governments with a set of unresolved problems that forced a steady decline in living standards. Venezuela has yet to succeed in resolving this boom-bust dependence on oil revenues, commonly referred to as the Dutch disease.[3]

By the 1990s, there were glaring discontinuities in Venezuela's policy process. Movement forward in reforming one sector was not matched by needed complementary changes in other sectors of the economy. With the deepening series of crises, the credibility of the political elite and of the state diminished. The once-strong political party system atrophied and came close to implosion, and domestic politics entered a stalemate. As the situation worsened in 1998, officials debated currency devaluation, but some believed it was better to leave that decision to the next government. Others believed that a credible devaluation was impossible to achieve, given the low esteem in which the government was held both domestically and internationally. However, the policy of defending the currency had some credibility because the central bank of Venezuela was viewed as one of the few efficacious institutions in the country.

The election of Hugo Chávez in late 1998 opened a long and uncertain road of political institutional change, but the economic program has undergone little concomitant adjustment. The decision to defend a semifixed exchange rate in 1998 was supported by the dramatic increase in oil prices at the end of that year and throughout 1999. However, underlying structural problems remain unresolved and oil prices are ever more volatile. As some observers point out, the currency regime must adjust to reality. When it does, both the political and the economic consequences could be severe and polarizing.

The four cases examined in the book confirm the difficulties inherent in the choice and management of the exchange rate in an international context of high capital mobility. Despite numerous attempts in the political economy literature to specify the most efficacious policy course for emerging-market economies to follow in choosing an exchange rate regime, the corresponding data on economic performance have yet to support any single approach. These four cases have shown that currency appreciation and exchange rate misalignment can readily occur under a fixed rate (Argentina, 1991–95) or under a more flexible arrangement (Venezuela, since 1998). Anchored rates, as employed in Mexico and Brazil during the early phases of economic adjustment, seemed to lose their logic once the initial goal of inflation reduction had been achieved. Although the shift to a floating regime in both countries set the stage for economic recovery, in neither case has the tendency toward exchange rate appreciation under conditions of heavy capital inflows been rectified.

In summary, these cases drive home the extent to which policy outcomes are, indeed, conditioned by domestic politics and the broader institutional backdrop. The choice of exchange rate regime clearly matters, but economic recovery and sustainable growth correlate most in those countries that have simultaneously pursued a prudent fiscal policy in conjunction with monetary restraint, and where policymakers have persisted in designing incentives to increase productivity and competitiveness. Each of these four cases offers valuable insights into the progress that has been made in coordinating exchange rate management with these other policy variables, and they all demonstrate that effective exchange rate management in the era of market reform still requires considerable fine-tuning. And, despite the trend toward greater exchange rate flexibility across the developing world, these cases suggest that the outcome is still far from certain. For now, it can be said that the political commitment to uphold a chosen exchange rate regime is clearly as important as the regime itself.

Notes

1. "Dollarization Takes Two Blows Abroad," *Latin American Weekly Report*, March 2, 1999, p. 101.

2. See Robert A. Mundell, "A Theory of Optimum Currency Areas," *American Economic Review*, vol. 51 (1961), pp. 657–65.

3. W. Max Corden, "Booming Sector and Dutch Disease Economics," *Oxford Economic Papers*, vol. 36 (1984), pp. 359–80.

Contributors

Eliana Cardoso is a resident scholar at the Egyptian Center for Economic Studies and formerly a World Bank lead specialist and senior adviser to Brazil's finance minister.

W. Max Corden is Chung Ju Yung Distinguished Professor of International Economics and Business at the Johns Hopkins University Paul H. Nitze School of Advanced International Studies (SAIS) in Washington, D.C.

Javier Corrales is an assistant professor of political science at Amherst College.

Timothy Kessler is associate director of the Partnership for Policy Dialogue based at Stanford University and the Carnegie Endowment for International Peace.

Riordan Roett is Sarita and Don Johnston Professor of Political Science and director of the Western Hemisphere Program at Johns Hopkins University–SAIS.

Carol Wise is an associate professor of political economy in the Western Hemisphere Program at Johns Hopkins University–SAIS.

Index

Acción Democrática (AD), Venezuela, 139, 149, 151
Alesina, Alberto, 132
Alfonsín, Raúl, 78
Alianza Democrática, Argentina. *See* Radical party–Frepaso alliance
Argentina: banking system, 18, 39, 103; capital flows, 1; currency board, 28–31, 39; economic performance, 8; exogenous shocks, 39; firmly fixed rate regime, 23, 28; fiscal reform, 29; inflation, 29; market reforms, 12, 106; multilateral loan package, 102; regulatory reforms, 97; resistance to exchange rate flexibility, 118; transmission of financial crises, 104–05, 164–65; transmission of Brazilian devaluation, 105–06; 165; weaknesses in economy, 118. *See also* Convertibility Plan; Currency board; Peronist party
Aias, Francisco, 151
Asian crisis, 36, 103; effect in Venez-
uela, 126; effect in emerging markets, 63, 126; effect in Brazil, 84; managed floating rate regime, 38; runs on depreciated currencies, 36
Aspe, Pedro, 48
Australia: managed floating rate regime, 38

Balance of payments: Argentina, 102, 105; Brazil, 79–84; and exchange rate anchors, 81; Mexican current account deficit, 44, 60–61, 66
Bank Deposit Insurance Institute (IPAB), Mexico, 58–59, 65
Banking system, Argentina, 18, 39, 98, 103
Banking system, Brazil: appropriation of seigniorage from, 77–78; credit under Real Plan, 76, 79, 81; economic recovery, 89; foreign banks and, 85
Banking system, Mexico: Bank Deposit Insurance Institute,